A POCKET HISTORY *of the* CIVIL WAR

OSPREY
PUBLISHING

TO MY LOVING WIFE, TINA
MY MOTIVATION, MY INSPIRATION, AND MY SUPPORT

A POCKET HISTORY
of the
CIVIL WAR

Citizen
Soldiers,
Bloody Battles,
and the Fight
for America's
Future

Martin F. Graham

Foreword from The National Civil War Museum

First published in Great Britain in 2011 by Osprey Publishing,
Midland House, West Way, Botley, Oxford, OX2 0PH, UK
44-02 23rd Street, Suite 219, Long Island City, NY 11101, USA

E-mail: info@ospreypublishing.com

A CIP catalogue record for this book is available from the British Library

ISBN: 978 1 84908 547 2

Page layout by Myriam Bell Design, France
Index by Alan Thatcher
Typeset in Adroit, Rosewood and MagestaScript
Originated by Blenheim Colour, Oxford, UK
Printed in China through Worldprint Ltd

11 12 13 14 15   10 9 8 7 6 5 4 3 2 1

Osprey Publishing is supporting the Woodland Trust, the UK's leading woodland
conservation charity, by funding the dedication of trees.

www.ospreypublishing.com

Contents

Foreword

Our nation, our States, and our fellow Americans are at the threshold of the Sesquicentennial of one of the most talked about, written about, and argued about periods of American history. In 1861, no American could have looked ahead to predict how the coming four years would change the course of the nation, nor could they imagine the importance their descendants would place upon this time.

As we begin the one hundred fiftieth remembrance of those defining years in the life of our nation, much more will be written about people, places, and events. From the first shots at Fort Sumter in April 1861 to the final stroke of a pen at the Appomattox Court House in 1865, we will relive and remember the American Civil War in these twenty-first century Sesquicentennial years.

A wave of new interest and revival of old enthusiasm will inspire book readers, battlefield visitors, museum guests, souvenir buyers, and living historians. Civil War-related websites, online searches, and social media will provide people with new ways to gain information and understanding about one hundred fifty-year-old historic moments. This age of electronic technology was not available in 1961 when America quietly recognized the passing of the Centennial of these events.

Every day at The National Civil War Museum, I look out of my window at the most panoramic beautiful view in Harrisburg, Pennsylvania. I can watch the weather change as it rolls across the Susquehanna Valley toward the Museum, positioned in Reservoir Park at the highest point in the city. Below, I can see our bronze statue of the "Moment of Mercy." It depicts a young Confederate sergeant, Richard Rowland Kirkland, engaged in an act of incredible compassion and courage during the horrific Battle of

Fredericksburg, December 13, 1862. The Moment of Mercy is the museum's signature memory and attracts thousands of "Kodak moments" every year.

Marty Graham's *A Pocket History of the Civil War* tells the story of nineteen-year-old Kirkland, who in the aftermath of the battle, secured permission from his commanding officer, gathered up as many canteens as he could carry, leaped the stone wall, and ran to the aid of wounded Union soldiers. This incident was repeated throughout the war by soldiers in both blue and gray. Told again here, it gives this story a new meaning and a fresh perspective.

Incorporating all of the fundamental information about the Civil War in one concise, easy-to-reference, and well-laid-out volume makes this an essential purchase for the Sesquicentennial Commemoration. Graham tantalizes the reader with appropriate quotes and statistical data that support his Civil War miscellany. He quotes famous Civil War leaders like Lincoln, McClellan, Longstreet, and Sherman. In addition, quotes from common soldiers, civilians, and newspapers drive home the stories and accounts of the battles and events of the period. The statistical figures, although known to the Civil War expert, are delivered in an easy-to-understand format and will be staggering to the novice Civil War reader. To reinforce this information for students and Civil War newcomers, Graham closes each chapter with a multiple-choice quiz to challenge their reading comprehension.

A Pocket History of the Civil War should be on every book shelf in America. Any Civil War enthusiast, no matter his or her level of interest, will enjoy the concise and fresh look that Marty Graham has put on a one hundred fifty-year-old subject. The battle accounts and personal stories will appeal to all readers who have an interest in the historical timeline of events.

David A. Patterson, CEO
The National Civil War Museum
Spring 2011

CHAPTER ONE

The Evolution of Soldiers

"I advise you, and as strongly as ever, to not come to war. I tell you you will repent it if you do, I do believe. You have no idea of what it is to be a soldier."

—Joseph Boyd, a Confederate Private, in an April 1862 letter to his brother[1]

WHY DID CIVILIANS GO TO WAR?

"The next day, April 14, was Sunday. The pulpits thundered with denunciations of the rebellion. Congregations applauded sermons such as were never before heard in Boston, not even from radical preachers .... Some of the ministers counseled a war rather than longer submission to the imperious South. Better that the land should be drenched with fraternal blood than that any further concessions should be made to the slaveocracy .... The same vigorous speech was heard on the streets, through which surged hosts of excited men .... Conservative and peaceful counsel was shriveled in a blaze of belligerent excitement."

—Mary Ashton Livermore[2]

Church bells rang throughout the North and South on Sunday, April 14, 1861, with a dual purpose: a call to church and a call to arms following the Confederate capture of Fort Sumter in the harbor of Charleston, South Carolina, the day before.

Thousands of men, young and old, flocked to recruiting centers. Many more volunteered by signing petitions circulated by prominent community leaders looking for a highly coveted officer commission. Others joined community militia groups being sworn into service. So many men volunteered that the Union and Confederate governments were hard pressed to adequately supply them. Newly inaugurated President Abraham Lincoln had requested Ohio Governor William Dennison to raise thirteen volunteer regiments, each with more than a thousand men. Dennison later wrote that, "without seriously repressing the ardor of the people, I can hardly stop short of twenty regiments."[3]

There were, of course, many reasons why so many men rushed to enlist. Among the most often cited reasons was a fervent desire to either abolish (Yankees) or preserve (Rebels) the institution of slavery in America. Many of these men also believed the war would last fewer than ninety days, and they did not want to miss out on the battle that would decide the fate of the nation. Many foreigners saw enlisting in the army as a means of endearing their people to this new nation. Some men, like Major Sullivan Ballou, who fought with the 2nd Rhode Island Infantry, were impelled to enlist by a faith in their governments, either Union or Confederate, as well as by the desire to preserve or fracture the country founded by their fathers and grandfathers.

"A pure love of my Country and of the principles I have so often advocated before the people—another name of Honor that I love more than I fear death, has called upon me and I have obeyed."

—Union Major Sullivan Ballou in a letter to his wife
a week before his death at First Bull Run[4]

Men from all occupations answered the call to arms, and many differences between the soon-to-be-enemies emerged in battle. The most striking is that the typical Northern enlisted man was better educated than his rural Southern counterpart. The level of education, however, had no effect on battlefield success. Once trained, the Confederate soldier became a formidable foe regardless of education. He showed a devil-may-care spirit in battle which was lacking in his foe. Yankee soldiers, on the other hand, demonstrated a greater sense of "group consciousness and team spirit."[5]

Federal defenses at Hiltonhead, Port Royal, South Carolina, during the American Civil War. (Mary Evans Picture Library)

TRANSFORMING CIVILIANS INTO SOLDIERS

"Every officer and soldier who is able to do duty ought to be busily engaged in military preparation, by hard drilling, etc., in order that, through the blessing of God, we may be victorious in the battles which, in His all-wise providence, may await us. If the war is carried on with vigour, I think, under the blessing of God, it will not last long."

—Confederate General Thomas J. "Stonewall" Jackson[6]

Turning this mob of civilians into fighting units was not an easy task. Neither government was prepared for the number of men who would answer the call to arms.

Prior to enrolling in the army, a potential recruit had to submit to a physical examination. This often was cursory, and as long as the recruit had teeth in the front of his mouth to rip open a cartridge or chew the rock-hard staple of the army—hardtack—he usually was given a passing certificate. In his memoir of the war, *The Story of a Common Soldier*, Leander Stillwell recalled:

"... the first step necessary was to be examined by the regimental surgeon as to my physical fitness .... I had previously heard all sorts of stories as to the thoroughness of this examination, that sometimes the prospective recruits had to strip, stark naked, and jump about, in order to show that their limbs were perfect. But I was agreeably disappointed in that regard .... He requested me to stand up straight, then gave me two or three little sort of 'love taps' on the chest, turned me round, ran his hands over my shoulders, back, and limbs, laughing and talking all the time, then whirled me to the front, and rendered judgment on me as follows: 'Ah, Capt. Reddish! I only wish you had a hundred such fine boys as this one! He's all right, and good for the service.' I drew a long breath, and felt much relieved."[7]

4

This was followed by signing the roll for the company he was joining. Before leaving the state to join an army, the new soldier was mustered into service by reciting an oath exclaiming his willingness to obey officers and fight against the enemy. Once mustered in, the company was assigned to a regiment and sent to a camp for outfitting and basic training. The formality of training often was skipped in later stages of the war. From mid-1862 to the end of the war, it was not unusual for a new regiment to be mustered into the service, rushed to a permanent command, and engaged in battle within a few short weeks.

In the months following the fall of Sumter, both sides suffered a severe shortage of supplies to clothe, arm, and support the new recruits, who often remained in camps for weeks awaiting supplies. One member of the 8th Ohio, Thomas Galwey, later recalled the regiment's situation three months after enlisting:

> "There was considerable delay in issuing us clothing and equipment. It was not until the second week of July that we were issued wooden guns, wooden swords, and cornstalks with which to drill and mount guard. We went to parade in our shirts, still not being fully uniformed."[8]

It was not unusual for sponsors, often men vying for election as officers of the companies and regiments, to spend their own money on clothes and arms for the whole unit.

While in training camp, enlisted men elected those officers of the regiment who were not appointed by the governor. These newly elected officers were usually as ignorant of military procedures as were the men they commanded. Those officers who were committed to their new profession studied *Army Regulations* in their free time to learn the intricate commands they would use until they were mustered out or became a casualty of this fraternal conflict.

THE ORGANIZATION OF NORTHERN AND SOUTHERN ARMIES

"Our armies are merely paper armies. I have 40,000 Cavalry on paper but less than 5,000 in fact."

—Union General William T. Sherman in October 1864[9]

Once in the field, Union and Confederate units were rarely at full strength. By the time a unit entered battle, it often was far below 50 percent of its regulation size. By way of example, and to demonstrate this difference, Figures 1.1 and 1.2 show the regulation strength of each Union and Confederate unit and the average number of men who actually reported for duty at the Battle of Gettysburg. Individual Confederate infantry units were larger than the Union's, but with fewer corps in each Rebel army.

FIGURE 1.1: UNION ARMY—INFANTRY				
	# of Infantry Units	# of Men Based on Regulation Size	Average # of Units at Gettysburg	Average # of Men in Unit at Gettysburg
Company		100		30
Regiment	10 Companies	1,000	10 Companies	300
Brigade	2 to 5 Regiments	2,000 to 5,000	4 Regiments	1,200
Division	3 to 4 Brigades	6,000 to 20,000	3 Brigades	3,500
Corps	2 to 3 Divisions	12,000 to 60,000	3 Divisions	10,400
Army	3 to 8 Corps	48,000+	7 Corps	73,000

FIGURE 1.2: CONFEDERATE ARMY—INFANTRY				
	# of Infantry Units	# of Men Based on Regulation Size	Average # of Units at Gettysburg	Average # of Men in Unit at Gettysburg
Company		100		40
Regiment	10 Companies	1,000	10 Companies	400
Brigade	3 to 6 Regiments	3,000 to 6,000	4 Regiments	1,600
Division	4 to 6 Brigades	12,000 to 36,000	4 Brigades	6,400
Corps	2 to 3 Divisions	24,000 to 108,000	3 Divisions	19,300
Army	3 to 8 Corps	72,000+	3 Corps	58,000

As the war progressed and more men entered the service, Union policy was to raise new regiments instead of replacing men in older regiments; Confederate policy was to continue to fill the ranks of the already-established regiments. In the final two years of the war, more regiments combined to form a single brigade because, by then, it was not unusual for a regiment to have fewer than two hundred men. By the time Union regiments mustered out after the end of their service, many had only a fraction of the number with which they first marched into the field. Confederate ranks naturally reduced as the number of replacements dwindled to close to nothing by the war's end.

Artillery and cavalry units were handled differently than infantry in each army. Union and Confederate artillery batteries often were combined into their own brigades. They also were detached to serve with individual infantry brigades. In the same manner, cavalry troops were attached to armies as regiments, but single companies often were detached, on both sides, to serve with separate divisions and brigades.

THE DAILY LIFE OF A UNION AND CONFEDERATE SOLDIER

"The Confederate soldier was peculiar in that he was ever ready to fight, but never ready to submit to the routine duty and discipline of the camp or the march. The soldiers were determined to be soldiers after their own notions, and do their duty, for the love of it, as they thought best. The officers saw the necessity for doing otherwise, and so the conflict was commenced and maintained to the end."

—Confederate Private Carlton McCarthy[10]

When one thinks of the soldier in the Civil War, thoughts of battles won and lost come to mind. In reality, however, soldiers on both sides spent more than 90 percent of their time in the regimented routine of camp. During the first few years of the war, months would pass between any significant engagements. This was especially true in the Eastern theater since there were two primary armies and activity was limited to Virginia, Maryland, and Pennsylvania. Ten months passed between the Battle of Gettysburg (July 1863, in Pennsylvania) and the next major action in the East, the Battle of the Wilderness (May 1864, in Virginia). In the Western theater, several Union and Confederate armies covered much more terrain.

In camp, a soldier's typical day would begin with Reveille at 5:00 a.m. in the summer and 6:00 a.m. in the winter, followed by Roll Call. The men would be given about thirty minutes to toilet, fix their uniforms, or catch a few more minutes of sleep. Breakfast Call sounded next, after which the men would line up for Sick Call or Fatigue Duty (cleaning up the company and regimental areas).

IN CAMP

I can't get 'em up, I can't get 'em up,
I can't get 'em up, I tell you.
I can't get 'em up, I can't get 'em up,
I can't get 'em up at all.
The corporal's worse than the private.
The sergeant's worse than the corporal,
The lieutenant's worse than the sergeant,
But the captain's worst of all.
I can't get 'em up, I can't get 'em up,
I can't get 'em up this morning;
I can't get 'em up, I can't get 'em up,
I can't get 'em up to-day.

—Variation of the words to "Reveille"
sung by some soldiers[11]

The number of men reporting for Sick Call increased daily, particularly at the beginning of the war and whenever the men were in camp for long periods of time. Although all soldiers were susceptible to diseases created by unsanitary living conditions, men from rural areas also were vulnerable to sicknesses common in the overcrowded cities of the North and South, such as measles and chicken pox.

Guard Mounting sounded at about 8:00 a.m. The detail for the next forty-eight hours of guard duty assembled and marched to its station. Each soldier on this duty was active at his station two hours out of six.

For those left in camp, Drill Call then sounded. This would continue until the noon meal. Soldiers then would have some free time, followed by additional drill until they were sent back to their quarters to prepare for Retreat in late afternoon. Retreat consisted of Roll Call, Inspection, and Dress Parade.

Supper followed Retreat, after which soldiers had additional free time until Tattoo (roll call and adjournment to quarters), followed by Taps.

Camp life could be routine and even terribly boring for the typical soldier. While campaigning, however, camp life was far from routine.

RATIONS

"What was hardtack? It was a plain flour-and-water biscuit. Two which I have in my possession as mementos measure three and one-eighth by two and seven-eighths inches, and are nearly half an inch thick. Although these biscuits were furnished to organizations by weight, they were dealt out to the men by number, nine constituting a ration in some regiments, and ten in others ... While hardtack was nutritious, yet a hungry man could eat his ten in a short time and still be

hungry. When they were poor and fit objects for the soldiers'
wrath, it was due to one of three conditions: First, they may
have been so hard that they could not be bitten ... They could
not be soaked soft, but after a time took on the elasticity of
gutta-percha [rubber]. The second condition was when they
were mouldy or wet, as sometimes happened, and should not
have been given to the soldiers ... The third condition was when
from storage they had become infested with maggots and
weevils ... When the bread was mouldy or moist, it was thrown
away and made good at the next drawing ... but in the case
of its being infested with the weevils, they had to stand it
as a rule."

—Corporal John D. Billings[12]

While in camp, a soldier's daily ration was distributed to him at each meal and consisted of a total of twelve ounces of pork or bacon or one pound, four ounces of salted or fresh beef; one pound, six ounces of soft bread or flour; and one pound of hardtack or one pound, four ounces of corn meal. Every one hundred men also were issued one peck (roughly eight dry quarts) of beans or peas; ten pounds or rice or hominy; ten pounds of green coffee, eight pounds of roasted or ground coffee, or one pound, eight ounces of tea; fifteen pounds of sugar; one pound, four ounces of candles; four pounds of soap; two quarts of salt; four quarts of vinegar; four ounces of pepper; a half bushel of potatoes when available; and one quart of molasses. Desiccated potatoes or vegetables sometimes were substituted for beans, peas, rice, hominy, or fresh potatoes. Small quantities of vegetables, dried fruits, pickles, or pickled cabbage sometimes were issued to prevent scurvy.

When on the march, a soldier was issued a day's or more worth of rations, depending on the plan over those next few days. The rest were carried in one of the hundreds of wagons that trailed soldiers on the march. A day's worth of rations on the march was considerably less than in camp and usually included one pound of hardtack; three fourths of a pound of salt pork; or one and one fourth pounds of fresh meat, sugar, coffee, and salt. Already loaded down with essential equipment on the march, the other rations available in camp were withheld from the soldier while in the field.

The Confederate War Department adopted the Federal rationing system at the beginning of the war, but was forced to reduce the amount of each item issued as the war progressed due to the shortage of supplies and money to buy them. When invading enemy territory or capturing Union supply depots, Rebel soldiers feasted on captured provisions. Throughout the war, the issue of ration supply was less of a concern for Union soldiers than it was for Confederates. Very few Northern farmers were impacted by the war, in contrast to their Southern counterparts, and supply lines for Yankee armies were usually well secured and well stocked.

ON THE MARCH

"No soldiers ever marched with less to encumber them, and none marched faster or held out longer. The courage and devotion of the men rose equal to every hardship and privation, and the very intensity of their sufferings became a source of merriment. Instead of growling and deserting, they laughed at their own bare feet, ragged clothes, and pinched faces; and weak, hungry, cold, wet, worried with vermin and itch, dirty, with no hope of reward or rest, marched cheerfully to meet the well-fed and warmly clad hosts of the enemy."

—Confederate Private Carlton McCarthy[13]

Although most soldiers found camp life to be routine and boring, marches were anything but. Long hours of walking in lines with uneven intervals of rushing and waiting in climates of intense heat or crippling cold through clouds of dust, miles of mud, or inches of deep snow were taxing on a man's psyche as well as his body. One of the best descriptions of life on the march was recorded by Union Private David L. Thompson of the 9th New York Volunteers:

"By daylight next morning we were in motion again—the whole army. The gathering of such a multitude is a swarm, its march a vast migration. It fills up every road leading in the same direction over a breadth of many miles, with long ammunition and supply trains disposed for safety along the inner roads, infantry and artillery next in order outwardly, feelers of cavalry all along its front and far out on its flanks; while behind, trailing along every road for miles—are the rabble of stragglers—laggards through sickness or exhaustion, squads of recruits, convalescents from the hospital, special duty men going up to rejoin their regiments. Each body has its route laid down for it each day, its time of starting set by watch, its place of bivouac or camp appointed, together with the hour of reaching it. If two roads come together, the corps that reaches the junction first moves on, while the other files out into the fields, stacks arms, builds fires, and boils its coffee. ... They march 'route step,' as it is called,—that is, not keeping time,— and four abreast, as a country road seldom permits a greater breadth, allowing for the aides and orderlies that gallop in either direction continually along the column. If the march has just begun, you hear the sound of voices everywhere, with roars of laughter in spots ... Later on, when the weight of knapsack and musket begins to tell, these sounds die out; a sense of weariness and labor rises from the toiling masses streaming by, voiced only by the shuffle of a multitude of feet, the rubbing and straining of innumerable straps, and the flop of full canteens. So uniformly does the mass move on that it suggests a great machine, requiring only its directing mind ... Half-way up the valley's western side we halted for a rest, and turned to look back on the moving host. It was a scene to linger in the

memory ... An hour before, from the same spot, it had been merely a scene of quiet pastoral beauty. All at once, along its eastern edge the heads of the columns began to appear, and grew and grew, pouring over the ridge and descending by every road, filling them completely and scarring the surface of the gentle landscape with the angry welts of war ... It was 3 o'clock when we resumed our march, turning our backs upon the beautiful, impressive picture—each column a monstrous, crawling, blue-black snake, miles long, quilled with the silver slant of muskets at a 'shoulder,' its sluggish tail writhing slowly up over the distant eastern ridge ..."[14]

On rare occasions, troops traveled by rail or water. For example, Confederate Lieutenant General James Longstreet's corps traveled by several rail lines to and from the Western theater following the

A group of unknown Confederate troops during the American Civil War. More than 500,000 P53 Enfields made their way to the United States for use by both the North and South. (Public domain)

Battle of Gettysburg, Pennsylvania, at the beginning of July 1863 to play a significant role in the Rebel victory at Chickamauga, Georgia, in mid-September 1863. Union Major General George McClellan's Army of the Potomac traveled from Alexandria, Virginia, to the tip of the Virginia Peninsula Campaign by boat in an unsuccessful attempt to capture Richmond, Virginia, in spring 1862 only to return in defeat to Washington (then called "Washington City" instead of "Washington, D.C.") by the same water route. By far, however, Union and Confederate armies traveled on their feet. It is estimated that the famous Rebel Stonewall Brigade, named after its first commander Thomas "Stonewall" Jackson, marched 4,222 miles during the course of the war.

THE FACE OF BATTLE

"The truth is, when bullets are whacking against tree-trunks and solid shot are cracking skulls like egg-shells, the consuming passion in the breast of the average man is to get out of the way. Between the physical fear of going forward and the moral fear of turning back, there is a predicament of exceptional awkwardness from which a hidden hole in the ground would be a wonderfully welcome outlet."

—Private David L. Thompson, 9th New York Volunteers[15]

War was declared and armies raised when politicians failed to resolve the states' rights and slavery issues through nonviolent means. In April 1861, men rushed to recruiting stations to enlist so that they would not miss the decisive battle that would decide the fate of the United States. They need not have worried, however, because there would be plenty of time for fighting. What these new recruits discovered during long years of campaigning was that their time on a battlefield would be very short and very intense.

The life of a soldier was generally a progression of camping and marching, occasionally broken by a few minutes of desperate fighting in battles or skirmishes. Throughout all of 1861, only one major battle was fought in the Eastern theater: First Bull Run. The next major infantry engagement in Virginia was almost a year later during the Battle of Seven Pines on May 31, 1862. From that day to the end of the year, only nine more major battles were fought in the East. Six of those battles occurred between June 25 and July 1.

There were only two major engagements in the Eastern theater during 1863: the battles of Chancellorsville and Gettysburg. The number of actions increased in both the Eastern and Western theaters, however, once Ulysses S. Grant became general-in-chief and instituted his policy of total war. From May 1864 to the end of the war a year later, the two sides were in almost daily contact.

The relatively few minutes spent in battle were intense and often felt like hours and days in combat. Camp life and long marches may have taken up the majority of their time, but experience in battle affected both Confederate and Union soldiers far more than anything else to which they were exposed.

"Some men, on the eve of battle, the most trying time in a soldier's life, will stand calm and impassive, awaiting the command, 'forward,' while his next neighbor will tremble and shake, as with a great chill, praying, meditating, and almost in despair, awaiting the orders to advance. Then when in the heat of the conflict both men seem metamorphosed. The former, almost frightened out of his wits, loses his head and is just as apt to fire backwards as forwards; while the latter seems to have lost all fear, reckless of his life, and fights like a hero. I have known men who at home were perfect cowards, whom a schoolboy could run away with a walking cane, become fearless and brave as lions in battle; while on the other hand men who were called 'game cocks' at home and great 'crossroads bullies,' were abject cowards in battle. As to being wounded, some men will look on a mortal wound, feel his

life ebbing away, perfectly calm and without concern, and give his dying messages with the composure of an every day occurrence; while others, if the tip of the finger is touched, or his shin-bone grazed, will 'yell like a hyena or holler like a loon,' and raise such a rumpus as to alarm the whole army. I saw a man running out of battle once (an officer) at such a gait as only fright could give, and when I asked him if he was wounded, he replied, 'Yes, my leg is broken in two places,' when, as a matter of fact, he had only a slight flesh wound. These incidents the reader may think merely fiction, but they are real facts."

—Confederate Captain D. Augustus Dickert,
3rd South Carolina Regiment[16]

"No one who has not witnessed such a scene can form any idea of the awfulness of that hour, the fearful screeching of the shells, the ominous buzzing and vicious whistling of canister and the endless 'ping ping' of the minie balls, while the reports of the musketry was one continual crash and, far above all, the thunderous tones of hundreds of cannon, completely drowned the encouraging shouts of the officers. The whole line was enveloped in a cloud of sulphurous smoke, almost hiding the regiments from each other and through which crimson flames from muskets and cannon darted fiery tongues. What carnage! Comrades fell all around you, mangled and bleeding; the colors go down, but are raised to fall again and again, the line moves forward with decreasing speed until when past the centre of the plain it finally stops, fires a few spasmodic volleys, wavers, breaks and flees to the protection of the bank from whence it had started. Then, without delay, it re-forms, moves up the bank and the tragedy is reenacted. Once more the scattered, remnants form a regimental line and are led forward with the same result."

—Sergeant Richard R. Foster, 19th Massachusetts Volunteers[17]

THE MEN WHO FOUGHT AND
THEIR TOOLS OF WAR

UNIFORMS

At the beginning of the war, the style of uniforms of volunteer soldiers on both sides of the conflict were determined primarily by the state from which their unit was mustered. There was such disparity in design and colors that identifying the enemy in battle often was difficult. Various Union and Confederate regiments wore either blue or gray uniforms, which often drew friendly fire during the heat of battle. By the end of 1862, both armies issued basic guidelines for uniforms, making it easier to keep soldiers supplied with replacement pieces in the field and to distinguish between friend and enemy.

> *"Every one was given a suit, hat, coat, pants and shoes—also shirts and drawers …. Most of the boys had never worn drawers and some did not know what they were for and some of the old soldiers who are here told them they were for an extra uniform to be worn on parade and they half believed it."*
>
> —Union Private Theodore Upson, August 1, 1862[18]

Though the basic items (hats, coats, pants, etc.) varied only slightly in style between Union and Confederate uniforms, quality varied quite a bit. In fact, the quality of a Confederate soldier's shoes was much worse than that of his Union counterpart. Rebel soldiers often looted the shoes of Yankee prisoners or the dead in areas controlled by the South after a battle.

Although many Civil War regiments wore unique accouterments, Figure 1.3 shows the standard issued items of the infantry uniform.

FIGURE 1.3: UNIFORMS

Item	Union	Confederate
Hat	Kepi—dark blue and made of wool, lined with cotton with a leather peak Hardee Hat (worn by Iron Brigade)—black felt with 3" brim	Kepi—same style as Union hat dyed gray or butternut Slouch Hat—thick felt with brim around circumference of hat
Coat	Sack Coats—short wool coat with straight back and no seem at middle with a simple turnover collar Frock Coats—single-breasted wool coat extending to the knee	Short-waisted sack coat or full frock coat made of coarse combination of wool and cotton (denim), dyed gray or butternut brown
Pants	Sky-blue trousers of coarse kersey cloth with high waists and round legs with 1" slits to fit over heavy shoes or boots; held up by braces (suspenders) or twine around the top	Same style as Union trousers, but made of wool and cotton
Underwear	Flannel and extending from waist to knees	Made of cotton or flannel with buttons of bone, wood, or glass
Shirts	Flannel or coarse wool with small turnover collars and three buttons	Same style as Union, but made of wool or cotton
Socks	Made of wool and poor in quality; often replaced by socks sent from home	Hand-knit wool or cotton
Boots	Jefferson Boots (Brogans)—ankle-high cowhide with a leather lace and soles either sewn on or fastened by wooden pegs or nails	Typically shoes of cowhide with broad soles and big, flat heels; could be sewn or fastened by nails or wooden pegs

THE INFANTRYMAN

"As infantry can move wherever a man can set his foot, can fight on all kinds of ground, gives the most destructive fire of all the arms, and is the least expensive and most easily instructed, it constitutes the great bulk of all large armies, and is decidedly the most important... The essential qualities of good infantry are: the ability to make long marches, with their full equipment, without straggling; accuracy of fire; confidence in their ability to use the bayonet—for this will prevent their breaking upon the

very near approach of a hostile line—coolness, intelligence,
determination, and mutual confidence in attacking or receiving
an attack; the ability to reform rapidly after a successful attack,
and to rally when driven back, either after a repulsed attack or
when obliged to retreat from a defensive position; the power of
enduring fatigue, exposure, and hunger."

—Union Major General George McClellan[19]

The same infantry command structure (company to army) was used in both Union and Confederate armies. Companies formed regiments, regiments formed brigades, brigades formed divisions, divisions formed corps, and corps formed armies. Within each unit of command were various ranks for officers, noncommissioned officers (sergeants and corporals), and enlisted men. Figure 1.4 shows the breakdown of this command structure at each level. Differences in rank for division, corps, and army commanders existed between Union and Confederate armies.

All soldiers had specific roles in camp, on the march, and in battle. The most dangerous—and at the same time the most honorable—role was that of color bearer, usually a sergeant.

Union regiments were authorized to carry a silk battle flag (the "Stars & Stripes") and a silk regimental flag of blue background with a painted eagle. The Confederacy lacked a common battle flag for their new nation. Throughout the war, about one hundred eighty different Rebel battle flag designs were carried onto the field or displayed across the South. The most famous of the many Southern flags was the one carried by the Army of Northern Virginia from November 1861 to the end of the war, called the Confederate Battle Flag. It was made of a wool or cotton material and had a blue "X" on a red field with thirteen white stars inside the blue stripes.

Troops used regimental flags to locate their units in camp, on the march, and in the heat of battle. Color sergeants typically carried the flags and were accompanied by a color guard whose job it was to protect the flag from falling into enemy hands, considered

FIGURE 1.4: UNION AND CONFEDERATE INFANTRY RANKS[20]		
Rank	Unit of Command	# of Men with This Rank in the Unit
Captain	Company	1
First Lieutenant	Company	1
Second Lieutenant	Company	1
First Sergeant	Company	1
Sergeant	Company	4
Corporal	Company	8
Musician	Company	2
Wagoner	Company	1
Private	Company	82
Colonel	Regiment	1
Lieutenant Colonel	Regiment	1
Major	Regiment	1
Sergeant-Major	Regiment	1
Quartermaster Sergeant	Regiment	1
Commissary Sergeant	Regiment	1
Adjutant	Regiment	1
Quartermaster	Regiment	1
Surgeon (Major)	Regiment	1
Chaplain	Regiment	1
Hospital Steward	Regiment	1
Principal Musician	Regiment	2
Assistant Surgeon	Regiment	2
Brigadier General	Brigade	1
Brigadier or Major General	Division—Union	1
Major General	Division—Confederate	1
Major General	Corps—Union	1
Lieutenant General	Corps—Confederate	1
Major General	Army—Union	1
General	Army—Confederate	1

an unforgivable disgrace. Because of their importance in providing order to units in battle, the color bearer was a vulnerable, popular enemy target. As Mary Livermore, a Union nurse, remembered in her memoir of the war:

"The fatality that attended the color-bearers, officers, and men of (the 24th Michigan Volunteers) at the battle of Gettysburg was very great... It carried into this battle only a state flag, which was presented to the regiment by the citizens of Detroit. This was carried by Color-Bearer Abel G. Peck, a tall, straight, handsome man, and as brave soldier as ever gave up his life for his country. He was instantly killed almost at the beginning of the famous charge of the Iron Brigade. The flag was then seized by Private Thomas B. Ballou, who was desperately wounded immediately after, and died a few weeks later. The flag was then carried by Private August Ernst, who was instantly killed. Corporal Andrew Wagner then took the colors and carried them until shot through the breast, from the effects of which he died about a year after the close of the war.

When Corporal Wagner fell, Colonel Henry A. Morrill took the flag, and gallantly attempted to rally the few survivors of the regiment. But Private William Kelly insisted on carrying it, saying to Colonel Morrill, 'You shall not carry the flag while I am alive.' The gallant fellow held it aloft and almost instantly fell, shot through the heart. Private L. Spaulding then took the flag from the hands of Kelly, and carried it until he was himself badly wounded. Colonel Morrill again seized the flag, and was soon after shot in the head and carried from the field.

After the fall of Colonel Morrill, the flag was carried by a soldier whose name has never been ascertained. He was seen by Captain Edwards—who was now in command of the regiment—lying upon the ground badly wounded, grasping the flag in his hands. Captain Edwards took the flag from him and carried it himself until the few men left of the regiment fell back and reached Culp's Hill. Captain Edwards is the only man who is known to have carried the flag that day, who was not killed or wounded."[21]

INFANTRY EQUIPMENT

"The knapsack ... is an unwieldy burden with its rough coarse contents of flannel and sole-leather and sometimes twenty rounds of ammunition extra. Mixed in with these regulation essentials, like beatitudes, are photographs, cards, 'housewife,' Testament, pens, ink, paper, and oftentimes stolen truck enough to load a mule. All this crowned with a double wool blanket and shelter tent rolled in a rubber blanket."

—Union Major Abner R. Small[22]

The list of equipment shown in Figure 1.5 shows the regulation issue for infantrymen on both sides. On their first march as raw recruits, soldiers carried all this equipment and more, including items they brought from home. This could add up to more than fifty or sixty pounds, not including a rifle. It was not long before weary soldiers began to discard equipment and personal items to lighten the load, typically carrying only their rifle, bayonet, caps, ammunition, blanket, canteen, and rations while on the march. They would restock once they settled into a permanent camp.

INFANTRY WEAPONS

"Plain smooth-bore Springfield muskets soon became Springfield rifles, and directly the process of rifling was applied to cannon of various calibres. Then, muzzle-loading rifles became breech-loading; and from a breech-loader for a single cartridge the capacity was increased, until some of the cavalry regiments that took the field in 1864 went equipped with Henry's sixteen-shooters [actually fifteen shot], a breech-loading rifle, which the Rebels said the Yanks loaded in the morning and fired all day."

—Corporal John D. Billings[23]

FIGURE 1.5: EQUIPMENT

Item	Union	Confederate
Knapsack	Made of black rubberized cloth or painted cotton cloth or canvas. A blanket roll, poncho, portion of shelter tent, oil cloth, and personal items were either strapped on it or stored inside. Fully packed, it would weigh between 30 and 50 pounds and was carried on the back	Much like Union issue; in fact, many had picked up enemy knapsacks that were discarded during long summer marches as well as prior to and after battles
Blanket Roll	Pure or mixed wool and measuring 7 feet x 5.5 feet	Mixed materials and sizes. Often sent from home or taken from a dead friendly or enemy soldier
Cartridge Box	Heavy black leather pouches with tinned metal containers to carry up to 40 cartridges (powder and bullets). Carried across the shoulder on a long, wide leather strap. Dimensions: 6.8 x 1.4 x 5.2 inches	Heavy brown or black leather pouch to carry 40 cartridges. Carried across shoulder on a long, wide leather strap. The dimensions were similar to the Yankee counterpart
Cap Box	Heavy black leather pouches, smaller than cartridge boxes, to carry musket and rifle percussion caps. Strapped to a soldier's belt, it had two flaps with a lambskin lining. Dimensions: 2.6 x 1 x 2 inches	Like Union counterpart, heavy black leather pouch attached to belt with the same dimensions
Haversack	Generally a foot-square pouch of Russian sheeting or painted cotton cloth with a wide strap to hang from the shoulder. Contained everything that couldn't be carried anywhere else	Size and material varied between groups of soldiers; carried everything that was not in the knapsack or rolled up in the blanket
Canteen	Various types of canteens were used by Union troops; mostly made of tin and wood. Made large enough to carry up to 3 pints of water. One style had a pattern of 7 concentric circles and was called the "bullseye" canteen	Although tin canteens were produced, wooden canteens made from cherry and cedar wood were widely distributed
Bayonet Scabbard	Heavy leather sheath with metal tip that hung from the belt	Same design as Union scabbards
Cup	"Boiler" hung from canteen on the march	Also hung from canteen
Poncho	Rubber blankets that served many purposes: raincoat, ground cloth, shelter, etc. When rubber blankets weren't available, painted blankets often were substituted	Similar to Union issue. Popular items to be scavenged from enemy dead and wounded following a battle
Shelter Tent	Larger than 5 square feet, half-tents were attached together by a series of bone or metal buttons	Similar to Union counterpart

One of the greatest technological advances the Civil War soldier enjoyed over his predecessors from earlier American wars was the widespread use of rifling (spiraled grooves) in the barrel of his musket. Prior to rifling, musket barrels were smooth inside and fired round balls with an effective range of less than one hundred yards. The rifled muskets that most Union and Confederate soldiers used throughout the war increased the potential killing range to distances ranging from five hundred to one thousand yards. Very few soldiers took advantage of that range, however, due to the fact that the velocity of a Minié ball fired from a rifled musket is much slower than a ball fired from a smoothbore because of the friction expended as it twists through the rifling in the barrel of the gun. The faster the bullet fired from a gun, the less elevation was needed to reach longer distances, so rifled

FIGURE 1.6: CIVIL WAR MUSKETS AND RIFLES	
Muskets/Rifles	Specifications
Muzzle-Loaded Smoothbore	
Springfield Model 1842 Musket	Length: 57.75 inches Weight: 9 pounds Caliber: .69
Muzzle-Loaded Rifle	
Springfield Model 1855 and Model 1861	Length: 56 inches Weight: 9.25 pounds Caliber: .58
Enfield British Pattern 1853	Length: 55.3 inches Weight: 9.2 pounds Caliber: .577 (ammunition interchangeable with Springfield)
Breech-Loaded Rifle	
Colt Repeating Rifle Model 1855	Length: 50 inches Weight: 10 pounds Caliber: .56 # Rounds in Magazine: 5 & 6
Henry Repeating Rifle	Length: 43.55 inches Weight: 9.25 pounds Caliber: .44 # Rounds in Magazine: 15
Sharps Rifle	Length: 47 inches Weight: 8.75 pounds Caliber: .52 # Rounds in Magazine: 1

muskets would have to be elevated a great deal to reach targets at longer distances. Because most volunteers received limited time on firing ranges, they were unable to adequately determine the required elevation of their gun for long-range targets, especially in battle. The killing range for both smoothbores and rifled muskets in battle was about a hundred yards. Although some soldiers perceived an advantage in using rifled muskets over smoothbores in battle, there actually was little difference. Figure 1.6 details the types of muskets and rifles used during the war.

Whether their muskets were rifled or not, both types were loaded by ramming powder and bullets into the muzzle and down the barrel of the gun. Figure 1.7 details the major steps it took to load a musket or rifle. It took eighteen drill movements to load and fire a smoothbore musket and seventeen for a percussion rifle musket. At their fastest, soldiers were expected to fire as many as three rounds in a minute. In reality, that rate often was considerably less in the heat of battle.

FIGURE 1.7: STEPS TO LOAD A MUSKET/RIFLE	
1.	Place stock of gun on ground between legs with bottom of barrel facing shooter
2.	Remove paper cartridge from cartridge box
3.	Tear open cartridge with teeth
4.	Pour black powder down barrel
5.	Place the bullet in the muzzle, hollow end first
6.	Remove ramrod from under barrel and ram bullet down muzzle
7.	Half cock and remove percussion cap from cap box
8.	Push cap over cone with thumb and pull back hammer to full cock
9.	Aim and fire

To take advantage of the grooved barrels of rifles, soldiers used elongated bullet-shaped projectiles called Minié balls after inventor Claude-Étienne Minié. These bullets had a hollow cone-shaped base and were made of soft lead to make the bullet easy to load. Once fired, the bullet would expand and begin to rotate in the direction of the rifle's grooves. This rotation was the reason for the accuracy of the gun.

Soldiers with muskets and rifles used paper cartridges containing both the bullet and powder. As described in Step 3 in Figure 1.7, the paper cartridge was torn at the top using the front teeth before the powder and round were inserted into the muzzle. Soldiers became proficient in loading their guns while standing, kneeling, or even laying down. When fighting was anticipated, each soldier was issued forty or more rounds of these cartridges.

Another technological advancement in small arms prior to the war was the development of breech-loading rifles, which were easier to load and fired more rapidly than muzzle-loading guns. This was seen as both an advantage and disadvantage. Although the faster firepower could increase enemy hits, it was discovered that soldiers using these rifles were less likely to take their time to aim. Therefore, greater firepower increased the need for more ammunition but did not increase the effectiveness of the soldiers using them. Several Union infantry regiments were issued these breech-loading repeating rifles, but they were used primarily by the cavalry. Few Confederate troops used breech-loading rifles due to the lack of factories and materials to produce them. Most of those in use by Rebel soldiers were captured from the enemy.

THE CAVALRYMAN

"The cavalry is an indispensable part of every army. It not only takes part, as occasion demands, in general battles, but, with a due proportion of horse-artillery, is capable of independent action, even at long distances from the main body of the army. Upon it devolves to a great extent the duty of observing and discovering the positions, movements, and strength of the enemy, as well as masking those of its own army. It is capable of making extensive inroads into the enemy's country, and is usually employed to threaten and attack his communications, supply-trains, etc. ....

The employment of breech-loading small arms has added very much to the strength of cavalry .... To render cavalry efficient it is necessary that the officers and men should be of a superior order of intelligence, and that they should fully understand the care of their horses, which should be active and enduring. Officers and men should be excellent horsemen, skillful in the use of their weapons, and thoroughly instructed in the work of reconnaissance. It is really much more difficult to form reliable cavalry at short notice than to instruct artillery and infantry."

—Union Major General George McClellan[24]

The formation of cavalry units was similar to that of the infantry for both sides. Cavalry companies often were referred to as troops. Figure 1.8 shows the command structure within a cavalry company and regiment. Beyond these units, the cavalry were formed into the same brigade, division, and corps structure used by the infantry.

Although a Union infantry regiment had a regulation ten companies, a typical cavalry regiment had twelve troops. This differed from Confederate cavalry regiments, which had ten troops. Just like the infantry, few Union or Confederate regiments came close to placing a full complement of men on a battlefield, and the numbers became drastically reduced after each action.

The cavalry was the eyes and ears of an army. During the course of the war, the Union raised 272 cavalry regiments, while the Confederates raised 137. These numbers do not include independent companies or battalions. The responsibilities of the cavalry on both sides included:

✢ Scouting the enemy's activities during reconnaissance missions
✢ Screening the armies' movements from enemy observation
✢ Pursuing and harassing routed enemy forces
✢ Delaying actions in the face of attacking enemy troops

- ✛ Attacking enemy positions and cavalry forces
- ✛ Conducting raids behind enemy lines to disrupt communications, capture supply depots, destroy railroads, and, in general, wreak havoc on the enemy

Cavalry regiments often were divided into companies or battalions to provide troops for army, corps, and brigade headquarters for security and to act as messengers.

FIGURE 1.8: UNION AND CONFEDERATE CAVALRY		
Rank	Unit of Command	# in Troop or Regiment
Captain	Troop (Company)	1
First Lieutenant	Troop	1
Second Lieutenant	Troop	1
First Sergeant	Troop	1
Quartermaster Sergeant	Troop	1
Commissary Sergeant	Troop	1
Sergeant	Troop	5
Corporal	Troop	8
Teamster	Troop	2
Bugler	Troop	2
Blacksmith	Troop	1
Farrier	Troop	1
Saddler	Troop	1
Wagoner	Troop	1
Private	Troop	75
Colonel	Regiment	1
Lieutenant Colonel	Regiment	1
Major	Regiment	3
Adjutant	Regiment	1
Quartermaster	Regiment	1
Commissary	Regiment	1
Surgeon	Regiment	1
Assistant Surgeon	Regiment	1
Sergeant-Major	Regiment	1
Quartermaster Sergeant	Regiment	1
Commissary Sergeant	Regiment	1
Saddler Sergeant	Regiment	1
Chief Blacksmith	Regiment	1
Hospital Steward	Regiment	2

CAVALRY EQUIPMENT

"I do my best for my horses and am sorry for them; but all war is cruel and it is my business to bring every man I can into the presence of the enemy, and so make war short. So I have but one rule, a horse must go until he can't be spurred any further, and then the rider must get another horse as soon as he can seize on one. To estimate the wear and tear on horseflesh you must bear in mind that, in the service in this country, a cavalry horse when loaded carries an average of 225 lbs. on his back. His saddle, when packed without a rider in it, weighs no less than fifty pounds."

—Union Captain Charles Francis Adams, Jr.,
in a May 12, 1863, letter to his mother[25]

The most important piece of equipment to a Civil War cavalryman—even more important than his weaponry—was his horse. Before treating himself to any rest after a day of active campaigning, a cavalryman made sure that his horse was properly groomed, shod, and fed, requiring a daily ration of about fourteen pounds of hay and twelve of oats, corn, or barley. During the course of the war, the Union army supplied more than eight hundred thousand horses to its cavalry units. The Federal War Department purchased the horses from private breeders or on the open market. Unlike the Confederacy, there was never a question of the government having the money to purchase horses. Due to lack of funding and supply, a Confederate cavalryman was required to supply his own horse and received a monthly reimbursement from the government for its care. If his horse died, the soldier was given sixty days to replace it or be transferred to the infantry. Incomplete statistics make it impossible to determine how many horses Rebel cavalrymen used during the war.

Next to his horse and weapons, the most important piece of equipment for a cavalryman was his saddle. By far, the most popular in the North during the war was the McClellan saddle, developed by Union General George McClellan after time spent as an observer of the Crimean War from 1853 to 1856. He noticed that the lighter saddle used by Prussian cavalrymen was much easier on the horse and rider than the heavier model used by the U.S. cavalry. The War Department adopted his model in 1859. About half a million saddles were produced during the Civil War (later models of the McClellan saddle were used by the cavalry until the cavalry disbanded mounted units prior to World War II).

The Union cavalryman attached a number of accouterments to his saddle, including an overcoat, poncho, a curry comb, saddlebag, nosebag, picket pin and rope to secure the horse while grazing, and a hook that attached to the muzzle of his carbine rifle. Attached to both sides of the saddle and straddling the underside of the horse was a surcingle, which was a safety strap to secure the saddle to the horse in case the saddle girth or leather straps broke.

The Jenifer saddle, designed by Lieutenant Walter Jenifer of the 2nd U.S. Cavalry, was chosen by the Confederate War Department at the beginning of the war. It quickly proved unpopular with Rebel cavalrymen because its design and weight inflicted serious injury on a horse's back during active campaigning. It was replaced by a rough replica of the McClellan saddle. The imitation also proved to be unpopular with Confederate troopers who sought every opportunity to capture McClellan saddles from their Yankee counterparts.

CAVALRY WEAPONS

"We had been furnished with sabres before we left Abingdon, but the only real use I ever heard of their being put to was to hold a piece of meat over a fire for frying. I dragged one through the first year of the war, but when I became a commander, I discarded it."

—Rebel Colonel John S. Mosby[26]

30

The cavalryman's most important weapons in an engagement were his rifle and revolver. Although sabers were used in close-encounter engagements, employing effective firepower was the cavalryman's most important offensive and defensive strategy. Figure 1.9 presents a summary of the weapons used by the Yankee cavalry during the war. Few Confederate cavalrymen had breech-loading rifles unless they picked them up after battles or from prisoners as spoils of war.

FIGURE 1.9: CAVALRYMEN'S WEAPONS	
Rifles/Revolvers	Specifications
Breech-Loading Rifles	
Sharps Carbine	Length: 39 inches Weight: 7.75 pounds Caliber: .52 # Rounds in Magazine: 1
Burnside Carbine	Length: 39.5 inches Weight: 7 pounds Caliber: .54 # Rounds in Magazine: 1
Spencer Carbine	Length: 39 inches Weight: 8.25 pounds Caliber: .52 # Rounds in Magazine: 7
Revolvers	
Colt Army Revolver	Length: 14 inches Weight: 2.7 pounds Caliber: .44 # Rounds in Magazine: 6
Remington Army Revolver	Length: 13.75 inches Weight: 2.8 pounds Caliber: .44 # Rounds in Magazine: 6
Colt Navy Revolver	Length: 13 inches Weight: 2.6 pounds Caliber: .36 # Rounds in Magazine: 6
Remington Navy Revolver	Length: 13 inches Weight: 2.5 pounds Caliber: .36 # Rounds in Magazine: 6

LOADING CARBINES

While it took as many as seventeen or eighteen movements to fire muzzle-loading arms, it took just seven movements for most breechloaders and only four for the Spencer Carbine. Several of the movements were combined into more than one of the steps shown in Figures 1.10 and 1.11.

	FIGURE 1.10: STEPS TO LOAD A BREECH-LOADING CARBINE
1.	Wedge carbine between right arm and breast
2.	With right hand, move back catch and open lever revealing barrel
3.	Press cartridge into barrel
4.	Pull back lever and engage catch
5.	Half cock and remove percussion cap from cap box
6.	Push cap over cone with them and pull back hammer to full cock
7.	Aim and fire

	FIGURE 1.11: STEPS TO LOAD A REVOLVER
1.	Hold pistol in left hand with muzzle up and half cock
2.	Remove paper cartridge from cartridge box
3.	Tear open cartridge with teeth
4.	Pour black powder down chamber
5.	Place the bullet in the chamber and press down with thumb
6.	Turn cylinder until under lever
7.	Uncatch and lower lever to ram bullet in cylinder
8.	Repeat process until all chambers are loaded
9.	Remove percussion cap from cap box and push onto cone
10.	Repeat process until all caps are on all cones
11.	Lower hammer on safety notch
12.	Cock the pistol
13.	Aim and fire

CAVALRY IN BATTLE

As mentioned, the cavalry served many functions in the Union and Confederate armies. Cavalry units often were broken up in order to accomplish these tasks, which limited the number of all-cavalry battles during the Civil War. The largest such battle was the Battle of Brandy Station, Virginia, on June 9, 1863. In this day-long battle, more than twenty-two thousand men and horses fought a "spirited" contest, as Confederate General J. E. B. Stuart later described it.[27]

Early in the war, the Union cavalry had been embarrassed by the escapades of such Confederate cavaliers as General Stuart and General Nathan Bedford Forrest. But, as the war progressed, the Union cavalry began to show that it was no longer overmatched by its rival. Although the outcome of the Battle of Brandy Station—the opening salvo of the Gettysburg Campaign—was inconclusive, the performance of such Yankee officers as John Buford, George Custer, and Wesley Merritt marked a turning point in the mounted rivalry.

Major General Philip Sheridan assumed command of the Union Cavalry Corps of the Army of the Potomac in spring 1864, at the start of Ulysses Grant's Overland Campaign across Virginia. His force engaged Stuart's command in a series of fights that led to Stuart's death at the Battle of Yellow Tavern in Virginia on May 11, 1864. Although Stuart's loss was mourned throughout the Confederacy, by the time of his death, his cavalry was not the force it once had been due to attrition and the inability of the Southern War Department to adequately support its cavalry.

Because it took the Federals longer to realize the importance of cavalry in the Western theater, its improvement as a fighting force

One example of some of the escapades going on in the South is J. E. B. Stuart's raid around the Union army during the Virginia Peninsula Campaign in the spring and summer of 1862. As a result of this raid, Stuart's cavalry provided Robert E. Lee with valuable intelligence that aided in his defeat of the Yankees at the gates of Richmond in June 1862. Nathan Bedford Forrest performed similar raids against Union forces and supply depots in the Western theater.

took longer than it did in the Eastern theater. It wasn't until the end of the war that, under the direction of Brevet Major-General James H. Wilson, the Union cavalry earned some success and respect against its Confederate opponents. Wilson was named the cavalry commander of the Army of the Cumberland in November 1864 and immediately proved his worth as a cavalry leader. His greatest success was his raid through Alabama and Georgia from March to May 1865, which began with the surrender of Selma, Alabama, and ended with the capture of Confederate President Jefferson Davis on May 10, 1865. Davis had been attempting to escape to Texas to reestablish the Confederate government.

THE ARTILLERYMAN

"Next in importance [to infantry] is the artillery, whose work it is to open the way for, and cover the movements of, the other arms by destroying the enemy's defenses at long range, silencing his artillery, and demoralizing his infantry; or, at short ranges, to crush them by a rapid fire of case and shrapnel. It is also a part of its duty to cover the retreat of beaten infantry, and to assist in the operations of detached bodies of cavalry. There is thus heavy artillery, whose business it is to handle siege-guns and those used in permanent defenses, and field-artillery, who accompany an army in the field. Field-artillery is made up of three kinds— viz., the mounted batteries, whose cannoneers usually march on foot, but during rapid movements ride upon the carriages and caissons, and which serve with the regiment, division, and army corps; the horse-batteries, whose cannoneers are provided with saddle-horses, and which are especially intended for service with the cavalry; and the batteries of position, consisting of the heaviest field-guns, intended especially for action against the enemy's material defenses."

—Union Major General George McClellan[28]

ARTILLERY PIECES

Union and Confederate armies used many of the same artillery pieces during the war. Those models that Southern foundries could not produce were captured on battlefields following Rebel victories. A list of the primary artillery pieces and their specifications is shown in Figure 1.12.

FIGURE 1.12: ARTILLERY PIECES		
Cannon	Specifications	Ammunition
Muzzle-Loading Smoothbores		
12-Pounder Howitzer, Model 1857 Napoleon	Bore Diameter: 4.62 inches Tube Material: Bronze Length of Tube: 66 inches Weight of Tube: 1,227 pounds Powder Charge: 2.5 pounds Effective Range at 5°: 1,619 yards Effective Canister Range: 200 yards	Solid Shot Spherical Case Shot (Shrapnel)—filled with 78 musket balls Shell filled with black powder and set off by a fuse Canister—cast iron shot packed in sawdust within a tin cylinder
Muzzle-Loading Rifled Cannon		
3-Inch Ordnance Rifle	Bore Diameter: 3.0 inches Tube Material: Wrought Iron Length of Tube: 72 inches Weight of Tube: 820 pounds Powder Charge: 1 pound Effective Range at 5°: 1,830 yards	Spherical Case Shot (Shrapnel)—filled with 78 musket balls Shell filled with black powder and set off by a fuse (Hotchkiss or Schenkl shells) Canister—cast iron shot packed in sawdust within a tin cylinder
10-Pounder and 20-Pounder Parrott Rifled Cannon	Bore Diameter: 3.0/3.67 inches Tube Material: Iron Length of Tube: 78 to 89 inches Weight of Tube: 900 to 1,750 pounds Powder Charge: 0.5 pounds Effective Range 10-pounder at 5°: 1,850 yards Effective Range 20-pounder at 5°: 1,900 yards	Solid Shot Spherical Case Shot (Shrapnel)—filled with 78 musket balls Shell filled with black powder and set off by a fuse Canister—cast iron shot packed in sawdust within a tin cylinder
Breech-Loading Rifled Cannon		
Whitworth Rifled Cannon	Bore Diameter: 2.75 inches Tube Material: Iron and Steel Length of Tube: 104 inches Weight of Tube: 1,092 pounds Powder Charge: 1.75 pounds Effective Range at 5°: 2,800 yards	Solid Shot Shell filled with black powder and set off by a fuse

The loading and firing of a cannon took seven men as many as thirty actions. The primary steps are detailed in Figure 1.13:

	FIGURE 1.13: STEPS TO FIRE A MUZZLE-LOADING CANNON
1.	Vent covered by piece of heavy leather (thumb stall) over thumb
2.	Bore of cannon sponged to remove lit embers remaining from previous fire
3.	Artillery round placed in muzzle and rammed down bore
4.	Cannon aimed using elevating screw
5.	Cartridge carrying powder pricked by wire through vent
6.	Priming tube inserted into vent and lanyard hook attached to it
7.	Lanyard yanked to fire the gun

ARTILLERY IN BATTLE

Artillery was used primarily as a defensive weapon. In offensive actions, the role of artillery was to soften the enemy defenses prior to an infantry assault. Two examples of the effectiveness of artillery in defense are the Confederate use of artillery during the Battle of Fredericksburg, Virginia, on December 13, 1862, when Lee's troops were defending Marye's Heights, and the Battle of Gettysburg, Pennsylvania, on July 3, 1863, prior to and during Lee's infamous Pickett's Charge.

Confederate Lieutenant General James Longstreet had twenty days to prepare his defense west of Fredericksburg in anticipation of a Union attack. His artillery and infantry covered the area of the Union attack so well that when he asked his artillery commander, Lieutenant Colonel E. Porter Alexander, his opinion of the defense, the artilleryman responded "General, we cover that ground now so well that we will comb it as with a fine-tooth comb. A chicken could not live on that field when we open on it."[29]

By the end of the day on December 13, thirty thousand Union infantry had charged Marye's Heights, but not one man reached within a stone's throw of the Confederate position. "A fifth time the Federals formed and charged and were repulsed," Longstreet later wrote. "A sixth time they charged and were driven back, when night came to end the dreadful carnage, and the Federals withdrew, leaving the battle-field literally heaped with the bodies of their dead."[30]

The attacks on Marye's Heights had failed, and more than seven thousand Union soldiers were sacrificed in the face of one of the most effective combinations of artillery and infantry fire of the war. As Lee stated while watching the carnage at Fredericksburg, "It is well that war is so terrible, or else we might grow too fond of it."[31]

Longstreet and Alexander also were responsible for the artillery barrage that preceded the charge of Confederate Generals George Pickett, J. Johnston Pettigrew, and Isaac Trimble across a mile of open ground before the Union defenses on the third day of the Battle of Gettysburg. Longstreet had little confidence in the success of the artillery barrage or the charge, but was ordered by Lee to command the action. Lt. Col. Alexander commanded more than one hundred sixty guns when the cannonade began at about 1:00 p.m. His objective was to destroy the enemy's artillery and soften the infantry line. However, poor quality and a shortage of ammunition, among other things, contributed to the ineffectiveness of this barrage. As a result, the Union batteries suffered few casualties and were ready to open fire on the long line of attacking infantry. Just as at Fredericksburg, artillery was handled much more effectively in defense rather than assault. In fact, the cry "Remember Fredericksburg!" was heard being chanted along the Union line as they crushed the Confederate attack.[32]

TEST YOUR KNOWLEDGE ABOUT THE SOLDIERS WHO FOUGHT IN THE CIVIL WAR

1. Identify which of the following firearms are muzzle or breech loaded:

   a. Spencer   b. Enfield
   c. Sharps   d. 1855 Springfield
   e. 1842 Springfield   f. Burnside

2. Identify which of the following firearms is a "smoothbore:"

   a. Spencer   b. Enfield
   c. Sharps   d. 1855 Springfield
   e. 1842 Springfield   f. Burnside

3. Place the following in order from the smallest to the largest organizational unit:

   a. Division   b. Brigade
   c. Corps   d. Company
   e. Regiment   f. Army

4. What was the name for the three-inch biscuit thought to be inedible by soldiers on both sides of the war?

   a. Hardback   b. Smoothback
   c. Hardtack   d. Smoothtack
   e. Hardstack

5. How many men comprised a regulation Union or Confederate regiment?

   a. 5,000 men   b. 100 men
   c. 1,000 men   d. 500 men
   e. 250 men

6. On what date did Fort Sumter surrender to the Confederates?

   a. April 10, 1861   b. April 11, 1861
   c. April 12, 1861   d. April 13, 1861
   e. April 14, 1861

7. On the average, were Confederate brigades larger or smaller than Union brigades?

8. What is the estimated distance that the famous Rebel Stonewall Brigade marched during the war?

   a. 2,340 miles   b. 3,770 miles
   c. 4,222 miles   d. 6,730 miles
   e. 10,020 miles

9. What was the Hardee?

   a. Hat   b. Coat
   c. Pants   d. Jacket

10. Soldiers were required to have their front teeth to do two tasks. One was to tear the ammunition cartridges. What was the second?

   a. Whistle alerts while on duty
   b. Bite the enemy during hand-to-hand combat
   c. Smile in pictures
   d. Bite into a piece of hardtack

CHAPTER TWO

Key Battles and Campaigns of the War 1861–62

FIRST BULL RUN (MANASSAS)—
MEETING THE ELEPHANT, JULY 21, 1861

*"There is Jackson standing like a stone wall! Rally behind
the Virginians!"*

—Confederate Brigadier General Barnard E. Bee[33]

During the first major battle in the Eastern theater of the war near
Manassas, Virginia, Union troops commanded by Brigadier
General Irvin McDowell had driven three Confederate brigades
from Matthews Hill and closely pursued them for a mile to Henry
Hill where Confederate Brigadier General Thomas Jackson's
brigade was forming its line of battle. The newly formed Rebel
army was on the verge of destruction when Confederate Brigadier
General Barnard Bee attempted to rally his disorganized
command by drawing attention to Jackson, "standing like a stone
wall" (more about that later).[34]

This marked the beginning of a legend that has extended far
beyond the history of the war. Legend or not, it seemed only a
matter of time until the outnumbered Rebel force, attempting to
mount a desperate defense on Henry Hill, would be smashed by
the advancing Yankee troops.

It had been little more than three months since Confederates had
captured Fort Sumter and war was declared. Within weeks,
Northern states began sending volunteer troops to Washington City
to defend the Union's capital and quash the rebellion. The generals
in command of the army, including Union General-in-Chief
Winfield Scott, were older than sixty and considered unable to field
a large army. The command of these new troops, therefore, fell to
McDowell, and he made every effort to prepare them for the great
battle most citizens on both sides believed would decide the fate of
the nation. A soldier's first time in battle was called "Meeting the
Elephant," and the men in both armies began preparation for this
life-or-death event.

About twenty-two thousand raw Rebel troops had advanced under the command of Brigadier General Pierre G. T. Beauregard, the hero of the fall of Fort Sumter, from the outskirts of the Confederate capital of Richmond, Virginia, to Manassas Junction, a strategic railroad junction just thirty miles from Washington. Another eleven thousand troops, under the command of Brigadier General Joseph E. Johnston, were at Winchester, Virginia, protecting the Shenandoah Valley from a Union force a short distance to the north.

McDowell marched his thirty-five thousand-man army south from the defenses of Washington down the Warrenton Pike toward Manassas on July 16, 1861. He hoped to drive the enemy from its defenses along Bull Run, about six miles north of Manassas, and advance on Richmond. Anxious to witness the battle that would destroy the Confederacy, a number of Union civilians followed the Yankee troops.

Like the civilians of Washington, the Federal army approached this first major battle of the war as if they were on a leisurely camping trip rather than advancing toward a clash between armies. They were in no hurry and took their time marching south from the capital. It took two days for McDowell's army to reach Centerville, less than three miles from the Confederate defenses, and another three days to launch an attack on the enemy left flank. This gave Beauregard more than enough time to determine his enemy's intentions and to have all but a skeleton force of Johnston's command transferred from Winchester, via the Manassas Gap Railroad, to bolster his undermanned army. Once he arrived, Johnston assumed command of the Rebel army from Beauregard due to seniority. After the two officers consulted on the situation north of Manassas, Johnston agreed with Beauregard's plan to attack on the morning of July 21. McDowell, however, struck first.

At about 5:30 a.m., Union troops attacked the Confederate line at a stone bridge as a diversion from McDowell's primary target, the Rebel left flank. After a long, disorganized night march, it was not until 9:30 a.m. that the primary assault force of thirteen thousand Federals crossed Bull Run at Sudley Ford, virtually unopposed, rushed forward to smash into the enemy's left flank, and drove them from their defenses along Bull Run.

Quickly realizing that the attack at the Stone Bridge was only a demonstration, Confederate Colonel Nathan Evans left fewer than three hundred men to hold off about ten thousand of the enemy at the bridge and led the rest—fewer than a thousand men—west to bolster the Rebel left flank. Outnumbered by more than thirteen to one, Evans attacked the enemy at Matthews Hill, holding off the Union advance until two Confederate brigades, one commanded by Bee, came to his aid.

It took the numerically superior Northern army more than an hour to drive the Rebels from Matthews Hill back to hastily constructed defenses on Henry Hill. As the fighting raged along Henry Hill, both armies sent fresh reinforcements into the fray until about 4:00 p.m. when Confederate forces turned the Yankee right flank and spread panic across the disintegrating Union line. McDowell's army ran for its life and did not stop until it reached the Washington defenses. Mixed into this melee were the hundreds of Northern civilians who had come to watch what they had hoped to be the defeat of the Confederacy. Instead, they became part of a disorganized route.

Although his men had driven the enemy from the field in a panic, Johnston determined that his army was just as disorganized as McDowell's and decided not to pursue the fleeing Federals. But the fact that their army did not pursue the enemy through the gates of Washington did not dampen the enthusiasm felt throughout the South following this decisive victory. In contrast, politicians and citizens alike expressed concern across the North. They quickly realized this would not be the short war as they had hoped for, but a prolonged fight to preserve the Union. Little did they realize the length of time and amount of blood that eventually would be spilled until the fighting was finally finished.

A number of historians believe that General Bee's cry "There is Jackson standing like a stone wall!"[35] was not meant as praise, but as derision for Jackson's unwillingness to join the fight on Matthews Hill. Bee never had an opportunity to explain his remarks, for he did not survive the battle, falling mortally wounded with many of his men on the slopes of Henry Hill. No matter his intention, Jackson was given the nickname "Stonewall" by the troops present that day and would prove himself to be one of the most successful and famous commanders of the war.

Figure 2.1 lists the commanding generals, the number of soldiers engaged, and the number of casualties at the First Battle of Bull Run, also known as the First Battle of Manassas.

FIGURE 2.1: FIRST BULL RUN (MANASSAS)		
	Union	Confederate
Commander(s)	Brigadier General Irvin McDowell	Brigadier General Joseph Johnston Brigadier General Pierre G. T. Beauregard
Number Engaged	35,000[36]	33,000
Number Casualties	2,896	1,982

THE USS *MONITOR* VS. CSS *VIRGINIA* (THE *MERRIMACK*)— THE BATTLE OF THE IRONCLADS, MARCH 8-9, 1862

"But at daybreak we discovered, lying between us and the Minnesota, a strange-looking craft, which we knew at once to be Ericsson's Monitor .... She could not possibly have made her appearance at a more inopportune time for us .... She appeared but a pigmy compared with the lofty frigate which she guarded."

—First Lieutenant John Taylor Wood,
CSS *Virginia* (*Merrimack*)[37]

Throughout the day on March 8, 1862, Union soldiers stationed at Newport News Point in Hampton Roads, Virginia, watched helplessly as the Confederate ironclad *Virginia*, commanded by Captain Franklin Buchanan, nearly destroyed the fleet blockading the James River. That morning there had been five wooden Yankee warships in the harbor: sloop-of-war *Cumberland* and frigates *Congress*, *St. Lawrence*, *Roanoke*, and *Minnesota*. By the end of the day, the three that had not already sunk were sitting ducks for the *Virginia* when it returned the next day.

While moored near Fort Monroe that morning, the crews on the Union ships *St. Lawrence*, *Roanoke*, and *Minnesota* saw the *Virginia* enter the harbor and head toward them. They set sail to attack the enemy, but each of the Union vessels ran aground, becoming sitting ducks for the Rebel ironclad. The *Virginia* targeted the *Cumberland* as her first victim and steamed directly toward it. Shots from the *Cumberland* and *Congress* easily bounced off the slanted iron plates of the *Virginia*, which rammed the *Cumberland*, sinking the sloop-of-war.

The Rebel ironclad, with the assistance of other Confederate ships, turned her attention to the *Congress*. The commander of the Union ship, Lieutenant Joseph Smith, ordered his crew to ground the frigate in order to escape being rammed by the *Virginia*. The armor on the Rebel ship was so heavy that it caused a twenty-two-foot draft, preventing her from being able to approach a grounded ship. The *Congress* was an easy target for the shells of the Rebel fleet, however, as she sat helplessly in the harbor. An hour after her grounding, Smith surrendered his ship. As Confederate sailors assisted in the removal of wounded sailors from the *Congress*, Federal guns from shore opened fire on them. In retaliation, Buchanan ordered the *Congress* set afire with hot shot (heated cannon balls). The vessel burned throughout the day until her magazine blew up, sinking the ship.

Ebbing tide and nightfall ended the fighting for the day before the Rebels could destroy the remaining trapped Union ships.

Buchanan, wounded in the thigh during the fighting, decided to retire for the night, repair the slight damage the *Virginia* had sustained from enemy guns, and return the next morning to finish the fight. Union shot had riddled the smokestack of his ship and loosened several armored plates.

Within weeks of the start of the war, Union troops and sailors destroyed all supplies and ships that could not be removed from the Gosport Navy Yard at Norfolk, Virginia. One of the ships that burned and sunk was the USS *Merrimack*. In June 1861, Confederates raised what was left of the *Merrimack* to form the base for what was to become the ironclad CSS *Virginia*. Construction was completed in February 1862. Her hull measured 263 feet. Surrounding her deck and slanting at about 35-degree angles were 24-foot-high sides as measured from the waterline to the top. The outer shell of her sides was covered by 4 inches of iron

The close-range fighting between the rival ironclads, Monitor *and* Virginia, *on March 9, 1862, is captured perfectly in this engraving. The damage to the smokestack, deck rails, and boat davits of the* Virginia, *much of which was caused during the action the previous day, is clearly visible.*
(Courtesy of Ron Field)

plate with a backing of 2-foot thick solid pine and 4-inch thick oak backing. She had 4 gun ports on each side and 3 rifle ports on each end. Her deck was covered in iron. She was fitted with a 1,500-pound cast-iron ram on the bow below the waterline, and she carried 10 cannon.

When the *Virginia* entered Hampton Roads on March 9, the day after devastating the Union fleet, First Lieutenant John Taylor Wood and the rest of her crew were shocked to see Yankee engineer John Ericsson's USS *Monitor*, described as a "cheesebox on a raft,"[38] standing guard over the *Minnesota*. Work had begun on the *Monitor* in October 1861, but it was not until January 1862 that she was christened. She was commissioned in the U.S. Navy on February 25, 1862. The *Monitor* left Brooklyn Navy Yard on March 6, heading to Hampton Roads for her historic confrontation with the *Virginia*. She was 172 feet long and 41 feet wide. One inch of iron plating covered the flat, wooden deck, which rose only 18 inches from the waterline. A 9-foot high, 20-foot wide revolving gun turret, protected by 8 inches of iron plating, was centered on the deck. Two 11-inch Dahlgren cannon were housed in the turret. Although the *Virginia* had a 22-foot draft, the *Monitor*'s was only about 11 feet, allowing it freer movement than her Rebel adversary.

The battle between the two ironclads began at 8:45 a.m. and lasted about four hours. Each ship pounded the other, inflicting minor damage. Finally, when a Confederate shell wounded the *Monitor*'s commander, Lieutenant John Worden, the two ships disengaged, and the *Virginia* returned to Norfolk. The first engagement between the ironclads ended in a draw. This was the only confrontation between the two vessels.

Facing no further resistance, Union troops strengthened their position in Hampton Roads and began expanding their presence along the waterways. As they approached Norfolk in May 1862, retreating Confederate troops were forced to destroy the *Virginia* to prevent her capture. Soon after her adversary's destruction,

The wreck of the *Monitor* was discovered in 1973, and the site was designated The *Monitor* National Marine Sanctuary and a National Historic Landmark. A 1978 study, examining the possibility of raising the ship, concluded that such an attempt would do extreme harm to what was left of the vessel. Since then, only pieces of the wreckage have been recovered, including her propeller, steam engine, gun turret, cannon, and anchor, as well as personal effects of the crew. These are on display at the Mariners' Museum in Newport News, Virginia.

the *Monitor* sailed into Norfolk, where she remained until December 29 when she set sail for Beaufort, North Carolina. Heavy seas pounded the Yankee ship until about 1:00 a.m. on December 31, when she sank about sixteen miles southeast of Cape Hatteras, North Carolina, carrying sixteen members of her crew to their deaths.

Figure 2.2 lists the commanders of the two ironclads, the number of sailors engaged, and the number of casualties during the clash between the *Monitor* and *Virginia*.

FIGURE 2.2: *MONITOR* VS. *VIRGINIA* (*MERRIMACK*)		
	Union	Confederate
Commander(s)	USN Lieutenant John L. Worden	CSN Captain Franklin Buchanan CSN Lieutenant Catesby R. Jones
Number Engaged	*	*
Number Casualties	409	24

* = total figures not known

SHILOH—GRANT'S CLOSE CALL
APRIL 6-7, 1862

"As we left the boat together, Buell's attention was attracted by the men lying under cover of the bank. I saw him berating them and trying to shame them into joining their regiments. He even threatened them with shells from the gun-boats near by. But it was all to no effect."

—Union Major General Ulysses S. Grant the night of April 6[39]

At daybreak on April 6, 1862, the Confederate Army of the Mississippi, commanded by General Albert Sidney Johnston, forty-four thousand men strong, charged out of the woods near Shiloh Church, near Pittsburg Landing, Tennessee, taking totally by surprise the forty thousand men in the Union Army of the Tennessee commanded by Major General Ulysses S. Grant. By nightfall, much of Grant's force was driven back to Pittsburg Landing, behind defenses lining the Tennessee River. Union artillery and guns from two ships on the river halted any attempt by the Confederates to drive the battered Yankees into the water.

Following victories at Fort Henry and Fort Donelson in Tennessee one month earlier, Grant had advanced his army through Tennessee virtually unopposed. Johnston's troops occupied Corinth, Mississippi, about five miles south of the Tennessee border, to protect the railroad junction located there. When the Yankees reached Pittsburg Landing, only twenty-two miles northeast of Corinth, Johnston realized that it was time to strike to prevent a Union advance into Mississippi.

Union Major General Henry Halleck, commander of Federal troops in the West, had ordered Grant to halt his advance at Pittsburg Landing and wait for the Army of Ohio under Major General Don Carlos Buell before continuing the push to Corinth. Anticipating little activity from Johnston's Rebels, Grant and his commanders failed to take the necessary actions to protect their positions.

Johnston's plan was to drive the Union army away from the Tennessee River and the approaching Army of Ohio. The Confederate general had hoped to launch his attack on April 4, but poor weather and bad roads delayed the battle until Sunday, April 6.

Although pockets of Yankees put up a savage defense, Johnston was able to concentrate his troops and slowly push his army forward toward the Union works. By the end of the morning, it looked as if Johnston's plan would succeed, but his troops were still relatively untrained, and his commanders found it difficult to maintain control of their men in the dense powder smoke created by rifles and artillery and the nearly impenetrable forest.

Johnston had hoped to turn the Federal left flank, driving the enemy from the river, but found greater success against its right, which had the opposite effect of pushing the enemy line toward the river rather than away from it. The middle of the Union line, extending behind a dense patch of forest, proved most difficult to seize. It took the Rebels several hours to drive the enemy from this area, named the "hornet's nest."

I t is speculated that a dueling injury Johnston received in 1837 may have contributed to his death at Shiloh. He was shot in the right leg by Texas Brigadier General Felix Huston and suffered severe nerve damage, which had not totally healed by the start of the Civil War. Due to this injury, when he was shot in the right leg at Shiloh, he may not have realized the severity of his wound until he fell unconscious from the loss of blood. Had the wound been treated immediately, he might have survived to fight on other battlefields.

During the morning battle, Johnston was mortally wounded in the leg. By that afternoon, he had bled to death. General Beauregard, the hero of Fort Sumter and First Bull Run, took command of the Confederate army.

Grant, helpless to stop the Rebel onslaught, decided to form his line of defense at Pittsburg Landing, protecting the route that Buell's Army of Ohio would use. Along the river, he lined up fifty cannons as well as the gunboats *Tyler* and *Lexington* to protect this position.

By nightfall, Beauregard's army was just as disorganized by its victory as Grant's was by its defeat. The Rebel general ordered his commanders to reorganize their men, feed, and rest them so they would be ready to resume the battle at dawn.

Buell's army and a division under Major General Lew Wallace (author of *Ben Hur: A Tale of Christ*) arrived during the night, strengthening the Yankee army to about fifty thousand men. Believing an attack by his army, reinforced with fresh troops, would turn the tide on the Rebels, Grant prepared to strike the next morning. At dawn on April 7, his army launched an assault that drove Beauregard's defenders out of their trenches. Stubborn counterattacks by the Rebels slowed the Union advance, but the Confederates were unable to break the Yankee battle line. Once the Rebel army was driven back to the area of Shiloh Church, Beauregard realized that further defense would prove fatal, so he ordered a retreat back to Corinth. Satisfied with his success, Grant decided not to pursue the enemy.

By the end of the fighting on April 7, the two armies had experienced a combined loss of almost twenty-four thousand men killed, wounded, or missing. The greatest loss to the Confederacy was the death of Johnston. Confederate President Jefferson Davis considered the fifty-nine-year-old leader to be the most competent of his generals. Davis noted that Johnston's death "was the turning point of our fate; for we had no other hand to take up his work in the West."[40]

On the Union side, Grant had narrowly escaped failure. Had his army been defeated at Shiloh, it would have had a significant effect on the war. It is likely he would have been passed over for larger command and even may have been transferred to a less important position—just as so many of his unsuccessful fellow Union generals experienced during the course of the war. Instead of the ultimate hero and future president Grant became, he would have played a lesser role in the history of the war, and Lincoln would have looked elsewhere in his search for the general who could bring an end to the war.

The Battle of Shiloh had been, by far, the bloodiest battle of the war up to that point. Although bloodier battles would soon follow, the number of casualties at Shiloh had a great impact on the perception of the war by citizens on both sides. They discovered that war was neither a game nor a glorious adventure for the men who enlisted, but a bloody affair from which there would be few winners and far more losers.

Figure 2.3 lists the commanders, number of troops engaged, and casualties during the Battle of Shiloh, also known as the Battle of Pittsburg Landing.

FIGURE 2.3: SHILOH (PITTSBURG LANDING)		
	Union	Confederate
Commander(s)	Major General Ulysses S. Grant Major General Don Carlos Buell	General Albert Sidney Johnston General Pierre G. T. Beauregard
Number Engaged	65,085	44,699
Number Casualties	13,047	10,699

THE SEVEN DAYS—LEE TAKES COMMAND
JUNE 25-JULY 1, 1862

"I prefer Lee to Johnston. The former is too cautious and weak under grave responsibility. Personally brave and energetic to a fault, he yet is wanting in moral firmness when pressed by heavy responsibility and is likely to be timid and irresolute in action."

—Union Major General George McClellan to
President Abraham Lincoln on April 20, 1862[41]

Confederate General Joseph Johnston, one of the heroes of the Confederate victory at Bull Run, was seriously wounded during the first day's fighting at Seven Pines, Virginia, on May 31, 1862. Federal troops under Major General George McClellan were within miles of Richmond, and the general the Confederacy had hoped would defeat the Union army and advance on Washington was now severely wounded. No one realized or could even imagine at the time the positive impact Johnston's wound would have on the fate of the Confederacy over the next three years.

Confederate President Davis chose his military advisor, General Robert E. Lee, as Johnston's replacement to command the Army of Northern Virginia. Placing Lee in that vital position was met with something less than excitement throughout Richmond for Lee had never commanded an army in the field. While Commander of the Department of West Virginia, the field generals under Lee had failed to drive Yankee troops from western Virginia. Southern newspapers, particularly the *Richmond Examiner*, wrote scathing articles against Lee. It would not take the general long, however, to prove his audacity as an army commander.

Union Major General McClellan had some of his own proving to do. He was a superb administrator and deserved every credit for creating the formidable Army of the Potomac, but, once in battle, he was unable to properly command it. Known by friend and foe alike as overly cautious, McClellan waited twenty-four days after the Battle of Seven Pines to attack. It would be his one and only offensive action over the next critical seven days.

Due to McClellan's lack of activity following Seven Pines, Lee had more than enough time to strengthen his line of defense and plan his own offensive campaign. His plan was to seize the initiative from the enemy and force McClellan to react to the movement of the Rebel army. Lee would repeat this strategy time after time during the course of the war against a string of Union commanders.

Lee discovered that the Union Fifth Corps, under Brigadier General Fitz John Porter, was deployed north of Virginia's swollen Chickahominy River to protect the Federal rail supply line. Isolated from the remainder of McClellan's force south of the river, this unsupported command provided a target that Lee could not pass up. He planned to attack on the morning of June 26, but his strategy was disrupted when McClellan struck early on June 25.

Attempting to seize high ground east of Richmond from which to shell the Confederate defenses, McClellan sent a corps across White Oak Swamp, but stubborn Southern resistance halted his advance. Darkness put an end to the daylong Battle of Oak Grove, with the Union gaining only about six hundred yards of terrain. This was the opening salvo of the Seven Days campaign. Lee seized the initiative the next afternoon and did not give it up until he had driven the Federal troops back into northern Virginia and Maryland.

Three Confederate divisions crossed the Chickahominy and attacked the right flank of the Union Fifth Corps line along Beaver Dam Creek on the afternoon of June 26, but a stiff defense by Porter's infantry and artillery inflicted heavy casualties and repelled each Rebel assault. Even though he was able to hold off the enemy, McClellan feared for the safety of his supply line to Washington. He decided, therefore, to abandon the railroad and move his base to the James River. He ordered Porter to withdraw his corps to the east, away from Richmond, about five miles, ending any hope by McClellan that he could capture Richmond by siege. He spent the next five days fighting to protect his numerically superior army from defeat at the hands of the Army of Northern Virginia and its new commander.

In the Battle of Gaines' Mill on June 27, Confederate forces finally broke the Fifth Corps line and drove the Union troops across the Chickahominy River. Two days later, after McClellan had begun his retreat to the James River, Lee's army struck his rear guard at Savage's Station, pushing them back in a disorderly fashion across White Oak Swamp. Among the casualties of the Battle of Savage's Station were five brothers, a cousin, and a brother-in-law in Company E of the 5th Vermont. Only one of the seven family members survived the wounds suffered in the fighting.

The fifth battle of the Seven Days was fought near Glendale. Lee attempted to cut off the retreat of a portion of McClellan's army to the James River, but a stubborn defense by Yankee troops, with the assistance of the guns from Federal gunboats on the James, held off the Rebel attackers and preserved the line of retreat.

The final engagement of the Seven Days was in front of the Union defenses at Malvern Hill. The Confederates suffered severe casualties without gaining any ground in several disjointed attacks against the solidly entrenched Yankee line. Following this battle, McClellan retreated to a defensive position along the James River, protected from further Rebel attacks by Federal gunboats.

In less than a week since taking command, Lee had driven the enemy from the gates of Richmond and earned a reputation as a much-more-than-capable army commander. With McClellan's army no longer a threat, Lee turned his attention to another Union army, commanded by Major General John Pope, threatening the Confederate capital from the north. He would meet Pope on the same field that saw the First Battle of Bull Run.

One of the greatest ironies of the war is highlighted by McClellan's quote that Lee, "when pressed by heavy responsibility ... is likely to be timid and irresolute in action."[42]

The Union general could not have been more wrong in this assessment of his adversary. It was more accurately a description of his own timidity when approaching battle.

Figure 2.4 lists the commanders, the number of troops engaged, and the number of casualties during the Seven Days Campaign. Figure 2.5 lists the major engagements of the campaign and the casualties suffered by both sides.

FIGURE 2.4: SEVEN DAYS CAMPAIGN		
	Union	Confederate
Commander(s)	Major General George B. McClellan	General Robert E. Lee
Number Engaged	115,000	95,000
Number Casualties	14,643	20,074

FIGURE 2.5: MAJOR ENGAGEMENTS DURING THE SEVEN DAYS CAMPAIGN			
Engagement	Date	Union Casualties	Confederate Casualties
Oak Grove	June 25	626	441
Mechanicsville	June 26	561	1,484
Gaines' Mill	June 27	6,837	8,750
Savage's Station	June 29	919	444
White Oak Swamp/ Glendale	June 30	2,700	3,600
Malvern Hill	July 1	3,000	5,355

SECOND BATTLE OF BULL RUN— A FAMILIAR STAMPEDE, AUGUST 28-30, 1862

"It was Sunday [August 30, 1862]. The morning was cold and rainy; everything bore a look of sadness in unison with our feelings. All about were the disjecta membra of a shattered army; here were stragglers plodding through the mud, inquiring for their regiments; little squads, just issuing from their shelterless bivouac on the wet ground; wagons wrecked and forlorn;

half-formed regiments, part of the men with guns and part without; wanderers driven in by the patrols; while every one you met had an unwashed, sleepy, downcast aspect, and looked as if he would like to hide his head somewhere from all the world."

—Union Captain William H. Powell, 4th Regular Infantry
Regiment, in a letter to *Century Magazine* dated March 12, 1885,
describing the aftermath of Second Bull Run[43]

By August 1862, the war already was almost a year and a half old, and the Union had yet to win a significant battle in the East. As McClellan was regrouping his army on the James River of Virginia after being beaten—physically and psychologically—by Lee during the failed Seven Days Campaign, President Lincoln brought Major General John Pope to Virginia from the Western theater to assume command of the newly formed, sixty-three thousand-man Army of Virginia. His orders were to march on Richmond.

When Lee learned of the new army marching through Northern Virginia, he dispatched Stonewall Jackson with twenty-four thousand men to delay Pope until the rest of the Confederate army could arrive. Jackson had been lucky to defeat Pope in the Battle of Cedar Mountain on August 9, a prelude to the Battle of Second Bull Run. Days later, Lee joined Jackson with Lieutenant General James Longstreet's thirty-one thousand-man command.

Jackson marched his "foot cavalry" around Pope's right flank on August 25 and captured the Union supply depot at Manassas Junction, Virginia. Once he destroyed the depot, Jackson encamped his men near the battlefield of First Bull Run, where he had gained his famous nickname the previous year.

In the early evening of August 28, Federal troops, seeking Jackson, marched along the Warrenton Turnpike, not knowing that Jackson and his Rebels were less than a few hundred yards away. Once artillery shells began cutting through their column near the John Brawner farm, Pope and his Union soldiers realized they had found the enemy—or, at least, that they had found each other. The two lines battled for about two hours before darkness put an end to the action.

Pope renewed the attack the next day. Jackson had deployed his troops in a section of an unfinished railroad with his left flank resting on Bull Run near Sudley Springs. Throughout the day, the Union troops struck at different sections of the Confederate line in a series of disjointed attacks. They broke through the Rebel line several times, but were driven back by desperate counterattacks. Although outnumbered by as many as two to one, Jackson held throughout the day.

Even though Longstreet's troops had arrived during the fighting on August 29 and actually had joined in the battle toward the end of the day, Pope seemed unaware of the Confederate general's presence when he sent ten thousand Union soldiers to attack Jackson's right flank at 3:00 p.m. on August 30. As the unwitting Yankees charged Jackson's defenses, Longstreet's Confederates anxiously awaited the order to attack the exposed enemy left flank. The order finally came, and Longstreet's force, more than thirty thousand men, struck in what may have been the largest massed assault of the war. The Federal line melted in panic, much like it had done during the First Battle of Bull Run. Only a stubborn defense by a small group of Yankees on Henry's Hill saved the Union army that day and allowed Pope to finish his retreat from the field under the safety of darkness.

Lincoln had brought Pope east to save Washington, energize the Union army, and mount a legitimate campaign against Richmond. But in less than a week, Pope was relieved from command and sent back west. Second Bull Run was another demoralizing defeat for the Northern army. They had yet to beat Lee, and the leadership in Washington seemed unable to find the man who could do it. His choices limited, Lincoln gave his army back to McClellan, not because he had faith in the general, but because he knew the soldiers loved him. It would not be long before McClellan had another shot at Lee, this time, however, in a must-win situation.

Figure 2.6 lists the commanders, number of troops engaged, and the number of casualties during the Second Battle of Bull Run, also known as the Second Battle of Manassas.

FIGURE 2.6: SECOND BULL RUN (MANASSAS)		
	Union	Confederate
Commander(s)	Major General John Pope	General Robert E. Lee
Number Engaged	63,000	55,000
Number Casualties	13,826	8,353

ANTIETAM—MCCLELLAN'S LAST TEST
SEPTEMBER 17, 1862

"Here is a paper with which if I cannot whip Bobbie Lee, I will be willing to go home."

—Union Major General George McClellan after being given
Confederate General Robert E. Lee's Lost Orders[44]

On September 13, 1862, as McClellan's Army of the Potomac pursued Lee's Confederates across the Potomac into Maryland, two Union soldiers found a copy of the Rebel commander's orders wrapped around three cigars lying in a field. McClellan discovered that Lee had split his army into four columns, sending three of them, under Stonewall Jackson, to capture Harpers Ferry and the fourth to wait in Boonsboro, Maryland, until reunited with Jackson's force. When asked about the danger of splitting his force in close proximity to the enemy, Lee responded:

"Are you acquainted with General McClellan? ... . He is an able general but a very cautious one. His enemies among his own people think him too much so. His army is in a very demoralized and chaotic condition, and will not be prepared for offensive

operations—or he will not think so—for three or four weeks.
Before that time I hope to be on the Susquehanna."[45]

Lee was not mistaken about McClellan's character, but he was wrong about the condition of the Union army. The Army of the Potomac was not demoralized or in a chaotic condition following the failure of the Seven Days Campaign and the defeat at the Battle of Second Bull Run. On the contrary, they actually were ready for another fight.

In the hands of a more capable general, Lee's lost orders would have been a death sentence for the Army of Northern Virginia. However, McClellan commanded the Yankees, and he was not about to let the acquisition of Lee's plans go to naught. "I think Lee has made a gross mistake, and that he will be severely punished for it …," McClellan wrote to President Lincoln. "I have all the plans of the rebels and will catch them in their own trap, if my men are equal to the emergency."[46]

The Union army attacked Confederate defenders in entrenchments along South Mountain on September 14, the day after McClellan read Lee's dispatches. The Rebels held the gaps until about ten o'clock that night, giving Lee time to retreat to Sharpsburg, Maryland, and issue orders for Jackson to rejoin the army as soon as possible. If McClellan had pushed his troops in pursuit of Lee and attacked at Sharpsburg on September 15 or 16, he would have outnumbered the Confederates by almost four to one. True to his nature, however, he remained cautious and did not attack the enemy until the morning of September 17, giving Jackson time to arrive with a portion of his command after taking the surrender of Harpers Ferry. McClellan's odds were now reduced to about three to one, still enough to overwhelm Lee's men if he sent the majority of his army into the fight at the same time.

The Federal attack along Antietam Creek on September 17 took place in three stages during the course of the morning and afternoon.

McClellan's First Corps attacked the Rebel left flank at dawn. After two hours of fighting across Miller's cornfield and in front of the Dunker Church, neither side had gained the advantage. The Union Twelfth Brigade and a portion of the Second entered the fight later in the morning, but the continued stubborn defense punctuated with counterattacks bogged down the Union assault in front of the East Woods. Sporadic fighting continued on this flank until about 11:00 a.m.

As the fight on the Confederate left flank continued, a portion of the Federal Second Corps attacked the middle of the Confederate line entrenched along a sunken road southeast of the Dunker Church. This was the second stage of the battle. The fighting continued in front of this "bloody lane" from about 9:30 a.m. to 12:30 p.m., until the depleted ranks of the Confederate defenders melted in the face of mounting Union pressure.

The third stage of the battle took place in front of the Rebel right flank. Major General Ambrose Burnside had been ordered to feint an attack across Antietam Creek at about 10:00 a.m. to take as much pressure as possible off the Federals attacking the Confederate left flank. For three hours, four hundred Rebel infantry supported by two artillery batteries were able to delay Burnside's twelve thousand five hundred men and fifty guns from crossing Rohrbach's Bridge across the Antietam. Finally, after almost running out of ammunition and losing about half of the defenders in the fighting at what was later named "Burnside's Bridge," the Confederates withdrew, opening the way for the Yankees to storm across the creek.

Burnside's attack stalled for more than two hours southeast of Sharpsburg. Faced with heavy Rebel artillery fire, Burnside ordered his men to take the town and then cut off Lee's route of retreat across the Potomac. His plan came close to succeeding before the remainder of Jackson's army arrived from Harpers Ferry after an exhausting seventeen-mile march and drove into the exposed Yankee left flank. The Union line collapsed in the face of the Rebel charge. Unnerved by the arrival of these enemy troops, Burnside ordered his men back across the creek and requested more troops from McClellan to renew his attack. The Federal commander responded that he had no fresh troops, although his Fifth and Sixth Corps had not been engaged in the day's fighting. McClellan, remaining overly cautious, refused to release them, afraid that Lee would launch a counterattack along the Union line. No such counterattack came, and the fighting ended at about 5:30 p.m.

Lee kept his army in line east of Sharpsburg throughout September 18, attempting to entice McClellan to attack, but the Federal commander, satisfied with the results of the fighting the day before, stayed behind his own lines. Although McClellan's troops outnumbered Lee's by more than two to one, McClellan seemed pleased that his army had successfully stood up to the enemy, fighting them to a draw. Lee's army retreated across the Potomac that night.

Since the enemy had abandoned the field and returned to Virginia, McClellan claimed victory. But Lincoln was not convinced of the success. He traveled to Sharpsburg to meet with McClellan in order to discuss the battle and the Federal commander's plan to pursue Lee's army. Dissatisfied with his general's lack of active pursuit, Lincoln replaced McClellan on November 5 with Burnside as commander of the Army of the Potomac. Burnside's tenure as commander would be brief, however, spoiled by a body of water and a muddy march.

One positive consequence of the battle was Lincoln's decision to use it as the platform for issuing his Emancipation Proclamation, turning the war into a fight against slavery as much as a desire to reunite the Union. Lincoln had been waiting for a decisive victory before issuing the proclamation, but that goal seemed out of reach. In fact, it would be another nine months before the tide of war would turn significantly in the Union's favor.

Figure 2.7 lists the commanders, the number of troops engaged, and the number of casualties during the Battle of Antietam, also known as the Battle of Sharpsburg.

FIGURE 2.7: BATTLE OF ANTIETAM (SHARPSBURG)		
	Union	Confederate
Commander(s)	Major General George B. McClellan	General Robert E. Lee
Number Engaged	75,000	38,000
Number Casualties	12,400	10,300

FREDERICKSBURG—IT IS GOOD THAT WAR IS SO TERRIBLE, DECEMBER 13, 1862

"I have just read your general's report of the battle of Fredericksburg. Although you were not successful, the attempt was not an error, nor the failure other than accident. The courage with which you, in an open field, maintained the contest against an intrenched foe, and the consummate skill and success with which you crossed and recrossed the river in the face of the enemy, show that you possess all the qualities of a great army, which will yet give victory to the cause of the country and of popular government."

—President Lincoln's Address to the Army of the Potomac,
December 22, 1862, following its defeat at
the Battle of Fredericksburg[47]

But for the want of pontoon bridges, Union Major General Ambrose Burnside may have sprung a disastrous surprise on the marble man, Confederate General Robert E. Lee. "Marble man" was a nickname given to Lee during his West Point days due to his moral fiber. Within nine days of assuming command of the Army of the Potomac, Burnside set his men in motion toward the Rappahannock River and Fredericksburg, Virginia. His plan was to steal a march on the Rebels, cross the Rappahannock near Fredericksburg unopposed, and race toward Richmond.

Before Lee could ascertain his enemy's intentions, the leading element of the Union army reached the eastern shore of the Rappahannock on November 17, opposite Fredericksburg.

Impassable roads and bureaucratic red tape delayed the arrival of the pontoons. By the time they reached the river on November 25, Lee's army had four days—plenty of time—to prepare a twenty-five-mile defense running south from Fredericksburg.

Union engineers began laying the pontoons across the Rappahannock at 3:00 a.m. on December 11. With daylight came small-arms fire on the engineers from Confederate sharpshooters and infantry hiding in buildings along the river's west bank. In retaliation, Burnside ordered one hundred fifty cannon to fire on the defenders and the town. More than eight thousand shells fell on Fredericksburg, but they had little effect on the Rebels lining the river. The same volume of small-arms fire greeted the engineers as they tried to complete the bridge. In desperation, Yankee volunteers paddled across the river and engaged the enemy in a firefight until darkness fell on the city and Rebel defenders retreated to their lines west of the town.

Union troops spent December 12 crossing the river and extending a line from the town southward. Those soldiers in the

Confederate soldiers under Beauregard rally before winning a decisive victory over the Union army under McDowell. (Mary Evans Picture Library)

town spent the day looting and vandalizing empty houses and drinking any and all alcohol they could find. By the next morning, many were in little condition for the task that faced them that day.

Burnside's plan called for launching an attack on the Confederate right flank at dawn and, once his soldiers had gained the advantage, sending his troops in the town forward to attack the heavily entrenched enemy line west of the city. The attack on the Rebel right flank began at about 8:30 a.m. The enemy artillery and infantry put up a stubborn defense that delayed the Union troops. As they pressed forward, however, they discovered a six-hundred-yard gap in the Confederate defenses and pushed through the breech, only to be driven back by a desperate Rebel counterattack.

The fighting on the enemy right flank had already lasted almost three hours before the Union troops in the town began their advance from the western outskirts of the city, across a deep drainage ditch, and through more than four hundred yards of open ground toward and amidst deadly Rebel musket and cannon fire. The Confederates had spent several days preparing their defense along Marye's Heights in a sunken road, making their position impenetrable to a Union charge.

Burnside realized the strength of the Confederate line west of the town, and had planned on holding up his assault on this position until the enemy right flank had been turned, making the Rebel position along Marye's Heights vulnerable to attack. When the earlier fighting bogged down, the Union commander made the ill-advised decision to send his troops forward—leaving the cover of the town with disastrous results.

"Column after column issues from the streets of the city," one Union infantryman remembered, "and after deploying into line, advances across the open valley under the murderous fire, to lose their share of men in the vain attempt to carry those impregnable heights."[48]

From late morning to nightfall, seven Union divisions attacked Marye's Heights in as many as fourteen charges. Not one man, however, would reach the sunken road.

Major General James Longstreet, the commander on this portion of the field, later remembered:

"Our musketry alone killed and wounded at least 5,000; and these, with the slaughter by the artillery, left over 7,000 killed and wounded before the foot of Marye's Hill. The dead were piled sometimes three deep, and when morning broke, the spectacle that we saw upon the battle-field was one of the most distressing I ever witnessed. The charges had been desperate and bloody, but utterly hopeless."[49]

During the night following the Battle of Fredericksburg, Burnside could not help but realize that his attack was a tragic failure. He called a meeting of his commanders to discuss the plans for the next day. Everyone was shocked to hear Burnside propose another attack against Marye's Heights for the next morning. Their surprise turned to disbelief when Burnside said he personally would lead his men against the enemy position. Some of his subordinates believed that the losses of the day had such a psychological impact on their commander that he wished to atone for the failure by dying during his last charge. It took much discussion, but Burnside's staff finally talked him out of this suicidal act. He called off the assault and ordered his men to retreat across the river.

A little more than a month after the failure at Fredericksburg, Burnside proposed a plan to march his army around Lee's left flank and cross the Rappahannock River behind enemy lines to force Lee out of his entrenchments into a fight on open ground. President Lincoln reluctantly approved the plan. Early mild January weather seemed in Burnside's favor, but after the march began, four days of drenching rain bogged the Union army in a sea of mud. The campaign only lasted three days before Burnside abandoned it.

Within days of the aborted campaign, Burnside was replaced by Major General Joseph Hooker, who inherited an army which Lincoln had observed possessed "all the qualities of a great army, which will yet give victory to the cause of the country and of popular government."[50]

In the right hands, the Army of the Potomac would show it was equal to its Confederate counterpart. Lincoln, however, had not yet found the man to successfully command it.

Figure 2.8 lists the commanders, the number of troops engaged, and the number of casualties during the Battle of Fredericksburg.

FIGURE 2.8: BATTLE OF FREDERICKSBURG		
	Union	Confederate
Commander(s)	Major General Ambrose E. Burnside	General Robert E. Lee
Number Engaged	115,000	78,000
Number Casualties	12,600	5,300

STONES RIVER—
THE FIGHT FOR MIDDLE TENNESSEE
DECEMBER 31, 1862-JANUARY 2, 1863

"The results of the battle were not what we had hoped, and yet there was a general feeling of elation. One day, after we had gone into Murfreesboro, I accompanied General Rosecrans in a ride about our camp. We had come across some regiment or brigade that was being drilled, and they raised a shout, and as he rode along he took off his cap and said: 'All right, boy's, all right; Bragg's a good dog, but Hold Fast's a better.' This well expressed my feeling as to the kind of victory we won."

—Union Major General Thomas Crittenden[51]

While soldiers from the Union Army of the Potomac were battered along the slope of Marye's Heights outside of Fredericksburg, Virginia, on December 13, 1862, the situation in the West was more favorable to the Union cause. Major General Ulysses S. Grant had just launched his campaign to capture Vicksburg, Mississippi, and Major General William Rosecrans was about to begin his push to drive the Confederate army under General Braxton Bragg out of Tennessee.

Only two months earlier, Bragg's Army of the Mississippi had reached the outskirts of Louisville, Kentucky, before it suffered a strategic defeat at Perryville, Kentucky, at the hands of the Union Army of the Ohio. Lacking the resources to continue his campaign in Kentucky, Bragg had withdrawn all the way to Murfreesboro, Tennessee, only seventy-two miles north of the Alabama border.

Rosecrans advanced his army from Nashville and intended to attack Bragg's exposed right flank on the morning of December 31. However, Bragg struck first, smashing into the Union right flank and driving it back beyond the Nashville Pike. Stubborn resistance from pockets of Yankee troops and artillery, coupled with rugged terrain, slowed the Rebel advance.

The fighting concentrated on the Union center at the Round Forrest. Wave after wave of desperate Confederate troops failed to drive the Yankees from their position. In his after action report, division commander Major General John C. Breckinridge reported that Union troops:

> *"were strongly posted in two lines of battle, supported by numerous batteries. One of his positions had the protection of the railroad cut, forming an excellent breastwork. We had no artillery, the nature of the ground forbidding its use. It was deemed reckless to attack with the force present."*[52]

The fighting ended for the day in Bragg's favor, but with about nine thousand casualties. Rosecrans and his commanders considered a retreat back to Nashville, but decided instead to rest and regroup the next day, January 1, and prepare for action on January 2.

Neither side attacked on January 1, but Rosecrans had advanced part of a division across Stones River to occupy an elevated position that exposed a portion of the Confederate line. Bragg opened an artillery barrage on the Union position for a half hour and then sent Breckinridge's division forward to drive the Yankees back across the river. Colonel George Brent wrote the following account of the charge in his diary:

> *"The division moved beautifully across an open field to the [enemy] work. A murderous fire was opened upon them. The enemy had concentrated a large force there and had combined a concentric fire from his artillery upon it. Our troops nevertheless marched up bravely and drove the enemy from the hill. The left of the division improvidently crossed the river contrary to orders: it was driven back in confusion. In [the] meantime, the enemy in large force assailed the right of the division, and it was compelled to retire. The cavalry on the right were ordered to cooperate, but they were mere spectators. It was a terrible affair, although short."[53]*

The action had lasted less than two hours and gained nothing for Bragg's army. With the presence of the enemy on his flank, exhausted troops, word that Rosecrans had received reinforcements, and five days of rain threatening to cut off his line of retreat, Bragg ordered his army to fall back about thirty miles to Tullahoma, Tennessee, half way to Chattanooga, one of the most important rail centers in the Confederacy. Rosecrans did not pursue the Rebels, deciding instead to remain at Murfreesboro and prepare for the next advance along the Nashville and Chattanooga Railroad line to Chattanooga itself.

The result of the two-day Battle of Stones River was similar to that of the Battle of Antietam three months earlier. It was not a decisive victory for the North, but the Confederates were forced to withdraw from the field, this time surrendering Middle Tennessee to the North. With prospects looking grim in the East, Lincoln was quick to draw attention to any positive military results that he could. He would remember the results of Stones River and acknowledge how grateful he was about the victory eight months later in a letter to Rosecrans. "I repeat that my appreciation of you has not abated," Lincoln wrote:

> "I can never forget ... that about the end of last year and the beginning of this, you gave us a hard earned victory which, had there been a defeat instead, the nation could scarcely have lived over [it]."[54]

As was the case with most Union generals during the course of the war, however, Lincoln's praise was short lived. Little more than two months later, Lincoln confided in one of his secretaries that, following the Union defeat at Chickamauga, Georgia, when Rosecrans retired from the field before the battle had ended, the Union commander had seemed, "confused and stunned like a duck hit on the head."[55]

Figure 2.9 lists the commanders, the number of troops engaged, and the number of casualties during the Battle of Stones River (Murfreesboro).

FIGURE 2.9: BATTLE OF STONES RIVER (MURFREESBORO)		
	Union	Confederate
Commander(s)	Major General William S. Rosecrans	General Braxton Bragg
Number Engaged	44,000	34,000
Number Casualties	13,000	10,000

TEST YOUR KNOWLEDGE ABOUT
THE MAJOR BATTLES OF 1861-62

1. Many Civil War battles had more than one name. Match the names:

   a. Manassas
   b. Shiloh
   c. Murfreesboro
   d. Antietam

   1. Pittsburg Landing
   2. Sharpsburg
   3. Bull Run
   4. Stones River

2. Which Confederate commander was killed during the first day of the Battle of Shiloh?

   a. Pierre G. T. Beauregard   b. James Longstreet
   c. Lew Wallace   d. Albert Sidney Johnston
   e. Jefferson Davis

3. Which of the following battles was not part of the Seven Days Campaign?

   a. White Oak Swamp   b. Manassas
   c. Malvern Hill   d. Mechanicsville
   e. Gaines Mill

4. Who yelled to his men "There is Jackson standing like a stone wall!"?

   a. Nathan Evans   b. Joseph Johnston
   c. Barnard Bee   d. Pierre G. T. Beauregard
   e. Henry Hill

5. A portion of what Union corps attacked the sunken road, or bloody lane, during the Battle of Antietam?

   a. 1st   b. 2nd
   c. 3rd   d. 4th
   e. 5th

6. Put the following battles in the timeline order in which they were fought:

   a. Stones River
   b. Antietam
   c. *Monitor* versus *Virginia* (*Merrimack*)
   d. Second Bull Run
   e. Fredericksburg

7. Which Union general opposed Robert E. Lee at the Battle of Fredericksburg?

   a. Irvin McDowell
   b. Ambrose Burnside
   c. John Pope
   d. George McClellan
   e. William Rosecrans

8. On what hill were Confederate Brigadier General Thomas Jackson's men deployed when he was given his famous nickname during the First Battle of Bull Run?

   a. Matthew Hill
   b. Chinn Hill
   c. Roberts Hill
   d. Henry Hill
   e. Ambrose Hill

9. Which of the following Union ships was not at Hampton Roads when the CSS *Virginia* attacked?

   a. USS *Constitution*
   b. USS *Congress*
   c. USS *Roanoke*
   d. USS *St. Lawrence*
   e. USS *Cumberland*

10. Which of the following men built the USS *Monitor*?

    a. Franklin Buchanan
    b. John Worden
    c. John Wood
    d. Joseph Smith
    e. John Ericsson

CHAPTER THREE

Key Battles and Campaigns of the War
1863

CHANCELLORSVILLE AND SECOND FREDERICKSBURG—STONEWALL'S LAST VICTORY, APRIL 30, 1863-MAY 6, 1863

"I cannot express my regret at the occurrence. Could I have directed events, I should have chosen for the good of the country to have been disabled in your stead."

—Confederate General Robert E Lee's reply to a note
from Lieutenant General Thomas "Stonewall" Jackson,
notifying the commander that he had been wounded[56]

After the crushing defeat at Fredericksburg and the disastrous "Mud March," Major General Joseph Hooker assumed command of the Army of the Potomac from Major General Ambrose Burnside. Not only did he inherit an army that was aching for a chance at victory over Confederate General Robert E. Lee's Army of Northern Virginia, but Hooker also was the recipient of a plan that Burnside rushed into when the weather proved to be his main nemesis. So confident was Hooker that his plan would finally defeat the Confederate army that he told several fellow officers on March 29, "I have the finest army the sun ever shone on …. My plans are perfect, and when I start to carry them out, may God have mercy on General Lee, for I will have none."[57]

Due to excellent planning and intelligence, three corps of Hooker's army stole a march on the Confederates, marching northwest from Falmouth, Virginia, to Kelly's Ford on the Rappahannock River. The Yankees crossed the Rappahannock there on April 29, followed by the Rapidan River at Germanna and Ely's Fords, while two corps crossed the Rappahannock on pontoon bridges south of Fredericksburg. With enemy activity in his front and rear, Lee was unsure of Hooker's intentions. Uncertain from which direction the main assault would come, Lee decided to wait for more intelligence before committing his army to action. While he waited, he sent a division west on the Orange Turnpike toward Chancellorsville to determine the enemy's intent from that direction.

By May 1, Lee ascertained Hooker's intentions and sent Lieutenant General Thomas "Stonewall" Jackson's command west on the Turnpike to strike the advancing enemy troops. The two sides met on high ground east of Chancellorsville along the Turnpike near the Salem Church at about 11:30 a.m. The stubborn Rebel defense seemed to unnerve Hooker, who did not expect such resistance at this stage of the battle. Afraid that his advance column was at risk, the Union commander ordered his army to fall back to Chancellorsville and entrench in order to resist an enemy attack. Like the Union commanders McClellan, Pope, and Burnside before him, Hooker had given up the initiative to Lee, and the latter was ready to take advantage of it.

That evening, Lee's cavalry commander, Major General J. E. B. Stuart, brought news that the Union right flank was unprotected, the enemy having decided that the Wilderness terrain was impenetrable. Therefore, the Yankee command believed, it was unnecessary to guard that flank. Jackson and Lee devised a plan where Jackson would lead two thirds of the Rebel army in a twelve-mile march, screened from the enemy by Stuart's cavalry, across Hooker's front to strike the exposed flank. As evidenced numerous times since taking command of the Army of Northern Virginia, Lee was not afraid to take tremendous risks to gain the advantage.

Hooker and his staff inspected his consolidated line around Chancellorsville. With his infantry ready and his artillery united on his front, he had little fear that his position was in peril. In fact, when he received a report from his cavalry that an enemy column was seen passing along his front, Hooker believed that Lee was actually in retreat in the face of his superior numbers. Hooker and his generals failed to grasp Lee's audacity when confronted. They would soon find out, however, how intense Lee's boldness could be.

During the inspection of the line, Hooker's chief of artillery, Colonel Cyrus Comstock, called aside Major General Oliver Howard, whose Twelfth Corps was assigned the Union right flank, and asked about gaps in the corps commander's line. The general replied, "The woods are thick and entangled; will anybody come through there?" Comstock replied, "Oh, they may!"[58]

They did at 5:30 p.m. when Jackson's men poured out of the wilderness, screaming the Rebel yell and taking completely by surprise the unprepared enemy, who were relaxing over supper. The Confederates met with little resistance as they pushed the Yankee line back almost two miles to hastily formed defenses just west of Chancellorsville. Jackson continued to press his men forward until fog and darkness slowed their advance. At about nine o'clock, Jackson ordered his officers to regroup and prepare to continue the fight into the night to cut off the enemy's line of retreat.

While his men took their short rest, Jackson took several aides to the front to assess the situation. As his small band returned to their lines, nervous pickets from the 18th North Carolina, thinking the approaching riders were enemy cavalry, fired on the party. Severely wounded in his upper and lower left arm and his right hand, Jackson was carried to a house near Dowdall's Tavern, where a Confederate surgeon amputated his left arm. Jackson then was carried by wagon over an extremely bumpy twenty-seven-mile ride to the safety of Guinea Station, Virginia.

J. E. B. Stuart assumed temporary command of Jackson's corps and continued the fight the next morning with concentrated small-arms fire along his line and artillery fire from the high ground of Hazel Grove, which the Union troops had abandoned reluctantly on Hooker's orders. During the fight, a Rebel shell struck a column Hooker was leaning against while standing on the porch of the Chancellor House, knocking senseless the Federal commander and sending him to the ground. Although he mounted a horse soon after to help rally his men, an aide observed that throughout the day Hooker seemed lucid but detached. By ten o'clock in the morning, Hooker had determined that his situation at Chancellorsville was untenable, so he ordered a withdrawal across the Rappahannock River.

While the fighting continued at Chancellorsville during the morning of May 3, Major General John Sedgwick launched an attack on Marye's Heights west of Fredericksburg on Hooker's orders in a desperate effort to relieve some of the pressure on the Union troops around Chancellorsville. Capturing the sunken road, the site of the slaughter of many men the previous December, Sedgwick immediately pressed west along the Orange Turnpike hoping to attack the rear of Lee's line at Chancellorsville. His advance was halted the next day near Salem Church, and Sedgwick was forced to retreat to the safety of the Rappahannock River's north bank. The Federal troops at Chancellorsville also crossed the Rappahannock during May 5 and 6, ending Hooker's plan to destroy Lee's army. Upon learning of the latest defeat of his Army of the Potomac, Lincoln lamented to visitors at the White House, "What will the country say? Oh, what will the country say!"[59]

The Battle of Chancellorsville, 1863, by Kurz & Allison. It was here that General Stonewall Jackson was wounded. (/Classic Stock/C.P. Cushing)

Lee had just achieved the most decisive victory yet of the Civil War, but any feelings of success were short lived. Four days after the last of the Federals recrossed the Rappahannock, Lee learned of the loss of Jackson, his "right arm."[60] While recovering from the amputation of his left arm, Jackson had developed pneumonia. He died at 3:15 p.m. on Sunday, May 10. His last words were, "Let us cross over the river and rest under the shade of the trees."[61]

Figure 3.1 lists the commanders, the number of troops engaged, and the number of casualties during the Battles of Chancellorsville and Second Fredericksburg.

FIGURE 3.1: BATTLES OF CHANCELLORSVILLE AND SECOND FREDERICKSBURG		
	Union	Confederate
Commander(s)	Major General Joseph Hooker	General Robert E. Lee
Number Engaged	130,000	60,000
Number Casualties	18,000	12,800

GETTYSBURG—LEE TAKES THE WAR TO THE UNION HEARTLAND, JULY 1-3, 1863

"For every Southern boy fourteen years old, not once but whenever he wants it, there is the instant when it's still not yet two oclock on that July afternoon in 1863, the brigades are in position behind the rail fence, the guns are laid and ready in the woods and the furled flags are already loosened to break out and Pickett himself with his long oiled ringlets and his hat in one hand probably and his sword in the other looking up the hill waiting for Longstreet to give the word and it's all in the balance, it hasn't happened yet, it hasn't even begun yet, it not only hasn't begun yet but there is still time for it not to begin against that position and those circumstances which made more men than Garnett and Kemper and Armistead

and Wilcox look grave yet it's going to begin, we all know that,
we have come too far with too much at stake and that moment
doesn't need even a fourteen-year-old boy to think This time.
Maybe this time with all this much to lose and all this much to
gain: Pennsylvania, Maryland, the world, the golden dome of
Washington itself to crown with desperate and unbelievable
victory the desperate gamble."

—Southern novelist William Faulkner[62]

In the early afternoon of July 3, 1863, Union and Confederate artillery hammered away at each other along two ridges south of the town of Gettysburg, Pennsylvania. The sound of more than two hundred cannon was so loud it could be heard in Pittsburgh, more than one hundred fifty miles away. While the artillery dueled, infantrymen on both sides waited for the moment they all knew was coming: a charge by Rebel soldiers on the center of the Union line on Cemetery Ridge. Confederate troops lined up

The Battle of Gettysburg and the charge of the Confederates on Cemetery Hill, Thursday evening, July 2, 1863. (Private Collection/Peter Newark American Pictures/The Bridgeman Art Library)

behind Seminary Ridge and stole glances at the enemy position across the mile of open ground they would soon be called upon to cross. This was a desperate move by their commander, General Robert E. Lee, who hoped that two days of battle on the enemy flanks would open an opportunity for his men to finally break the center of the Union line. His troops waited anxiously for the guns to stop and the order to advance to be given.

By the morning of July 3, thousands of men already had been killed or wounded in a fight and at a location where neither commander had intended to wage battle. Following a string of strategic successes that included the Battles of Fredericksburg and Chancellorsville, Lee petitioned President Jefferson Davis for permission to invade Northern soil a second time. The first attempt ended at Antietam, Maryland, about eight months earlier. Lee hoped to replenish supplies that were difficult to find in Virginia by the second year of the war. He also hoped to threaten Philadelphia, Baltimore, and even Washington in an attempt to force the Union to sue for peace and to gain official recognition of the Confederacy by European nations.

On the Union side, following his disastrous defeat at Chancellorsville the month before, Major General Joseph Hooker's army had returned to its winter camp east of the Rappahannock River across from Fredericksburg. Hooker had lost the confidence of President Lincoln and his War Department, especially as he was slow to react to Lee's movement north. On June 28, Hooker finally was replaced as commander of the Army of the Potomac by Major General George G. Meade. The army continued after the enemy in a desperate attempt to remain between them and Washington.

When Lee learned that the Union army was in pursuit and had, by June 29, crossed the Potomac into Maryland, he ordered his divisions, which were strung across Maryland and Pennsylvania, to concentrate at Cashtown, Pennsylvania, at the eastern base of South Mountain and several miles west of Gettysburg. Before Lee could consolidate his command, however, one of his divisions engaged Union cavalry on the western outskirts of Gettysburg on the morning of July 1. When the fighting began, corps and division commanders on both sides rushed men into the combat. Before Lee or Meade could decide on the merits of the location, it was too late: The battle had begun.

Throughout the morning and afternoon of July 1, two Union corps of infantry and artillery formed a line running from west to north of the town. They put up a stubborn defense at locations with the names McPherson's Ridge, Oak Ridge, and Barlow's Knoll until their flanks were turned by enemy troops, causing the Yankees to seek escape through the streets of Gettysburg to a height called Cemetery Hill, located south of town. Lee ordered the attack on that position "if practicable,"[63] but his Second Corps commander, Lieutenant General Richard Ewell, believed the unknown disposition of enemy troops and artillery on the hill and on his left flank made the attack too dangerous. This decision often has been second-guessed over the years. Would "Stonewall" Jackson have attacked if he were in command? That is one of the great unknowns of the war.

The first day of battle was a victory for Lee's army, but it was by no means a decisive victory. Although Union troops were routed, the day ended with Northern troops well entrenched in a commanding position south of Gettysburg. It then was up to both commanders to determine what to do the next morning.

When Meade arrived on the field, he was satisfied with the line of defense his commanders had established. The Union right flank was anchored on Culp's Hill, southeast of town. From there the line formed in a fishhook across Cemetery Hill, running south from there along Cemetery Ridge to two commanding hills, Little Round Top and Big Round Top.

Reconnaissance during the night gave Lee an idea of the extent of the Union deployment. He was convinced that he should attack it the next day, but not all his commanders agreed. Lieutenant General James Longstreet favored shifting the line to the south, between the

Union army and Washington, therefore forcing Meade to attack over ground favorable to a successful defense. "Finding our object is Washington or that army," Longstreet told Lee, "the Federals will be sure to attack us. When they attack, we shall beat them, as we proposed to do before we left Fredericksburg, and the probabilities are that the fruits of success will be great." To that, Lee responded, "No; the enemy is there, and I am going to attack him there."[64]

Lee's plan for July 2 was to send Longstreet's Corps (minus Major General George Pickett's division, which had not yet arrived at Gettysburg) in a masked march across the Union front to strike the enemy's left flank, much like Jackson's march, which had proved so successful at Chancellorsville. Once Longstreet attacked, Ewell was to assault the Union right flank.

Longstreet's march took longer than expected because part of the line of march was exposed to a Federal signal station. Longstreet's men were forced to back-track and were not in position to attack until 3:30 p.m. Desperate, fierce, bloody fighting took place all along the Union left flank on Little Round Top, at Devil's Den, across the Wheatfield, in the Peach Orchard, and along most of Cemetery Ridge. When the battle ended, the Confederates had driven the Yankees back about a mile from Emmitsburg Road to Cemetery Ridge, but the Union line held. Ewell failed to attack until later in the afternoon of July 2, and his men failed to drive the enemy from either Culp's Hill or Cemetery Hill.

On the morning of July 3, the Union army was concentrated in a solid line along the fishhook pattern they held the day before, while the Confederates were stretched out in a long line that paralleled the fishhook. Meade had strong internal lines of communication, but Lee's army was so spread out that coordination from one end to the other was difficult, if not impossible. The Confederate commander was convinced, however, that his army, which had defeated the Yankees on almost every battlefield during the past year, was invincible and that it could drive the enemy from their position.

When Lee approached Longstreet with his plan to strike the Union center on Cemetery Ridge, his corps commander again proposed a march around the enemy left flank. Lee responded:

> "No. I am going to take them where they are on Cemetery Hill. I want you to take Pickett's division and make the attack. I will reinforce you by two divisions [Heth's under Pettigrew and Pender's under Trimble] of the Third Corps."[65]

"That will give me fifteen thousand men," Longstreet responded. He continued:

> "I have been a soldier, I may say, from the ranks up to the position I now hold. I have been in pretty much all kinds of skirmishes, from those of two or three soldiers up to those of an army corps, and I think I can safely say there never was a body of fifteen thousand men who could make that attack successfully."[66]

Lee was determined to attack, however.

An early-morning assault by Federal troops on Culp's Hill succeeded in driving the Confederates from their tentative hold on the east side of the hill. Then, two signal guns fired at about 1:00 p.m., were followed by one hundred fifty Confederate cannon. The exchange of cannon fire continued for almost two hours before the time came for the Rebel infantry to attack. "As [Pickett] came up he asked if the time for his advance had come," Longstreet later wrote:

> "I was convinced that he would be leading his troops to needless slaughter, and did not speak. He repeated the question, and without opening my lips I bowed in answer. In a determined voice Pickett said: 'Sir, I shall lead my division forward.'"[67]

The Confederate infantry advanced across the open ground toward a copse of trees that stood prominently on Cemetery Ridge. Union artillery cut large gaps in the Rebel line as they advanced. Once they reached the Emmitsburg Road, hundreds of Union rifles opened on the charging enemy. In the face of this destructive fire, Confederate troops continued to advance. A large group led by Brigadier General Lewis Armistead even briefly pierced the Union line, but, as Armistead lay dying from a mortal wound, Union reinforcements closed the breech. Those Rebels who had survived death, wounds, or capture made their way slowly back to the Confederate line along Seminary Ridge. Of the twelve to fourteen thousand men who actually made the charge, it is estimated that almost half failed to return to their line. As the remnants of Pickett's division returned, Lee was heard to say, "It was all my fault; get together, and let us do the best we can toward saving that which is left us."[68]

Lee immediately began to prepare for a Union attack that never came. His men, exhausted but not broken, waited the next day, but still no Union attack was attempted. Finally, Lee began his retreat back to Virginia in the rain on the evening of July 5. Thus ended his last attempt at victory on Northern soil. The war would last almost two more years, but this was the last time Lee had the resources to launch a major offensive against his Union adversary.

Meade was happy to survive three days of bloody fighting. Satisfied in spending the next two days licking his wounds, he would not begin his pursuit of Lee's army until July 6, an act for which he was roundly criticized. For the citizens of the North, however, the news of the Union victory at Gettysburg, along with the surrender of Vicksburg, gave them a much-needed joyous July 4 celebration.

Figure 3.2 lists the commanders, the number of troops engaged, and the number of casualties during the Battle of Gettysburg.

FIGURE 3.2: BATTLE OF GETTYSBURG		
	Union	Confederate
Commander(s)	Major General George G. Meade	General Robert E. Lee
Number Engaged	95,000	75,000
Number Casualties	23,000	28,000

SIEGE OF VICKSBURG—GRANT CONQUERS THE GREAT MISSISSIPPI, MAY 18-JULY 4, 1863

"If you can't feed us, you had better surrender us—horrible as the idea is—than suffer this noble army to disgrace themselves by desertion. I tell you plainly men are not going to lie here and perish .... You had better heed a warning voice, though it is the voice of a private soldier. This army is now ripe for mutiny unless it can be fed."

—Letter received by Lieutenant General John C. Pemberton on June 28, 1863, signed "Many Soldiers in the Trenches"[69]

Major General Ulysses S. Grant's operation against Vicksburg, Mississippi, began inauspiciously in December 1862 with a defeat at Chickasaw Bayou, Mississippi, north of Vicksburg. His second attempt to capture Vicksburg by direct assault from the north also ended in defeat and proved very costly when his force of thirty-two thousand men was stopped by less than half their number. The city was protected on the east by Rebel entrenchments and on the west by the Mississippi River. If Grant was to take the city, it would have to be from the south.

Vicksburg was the last major Rebel stronghold on the Mississippi River. Confederate President Jefferson Davis had proclaimed its importance to the Confederacy: "Vicksburg is the nail-head that holds the South's two halves together."[70] In his memoirs, Grant stated why he spent more than seven months capturing the "Gibraltar of the South:"[71]

"Vicksburg was important to the enemy because it occupied the first high ground coming close to the river below Memphis. From there a railroad runs east, connecting with other roads leading to all points of the Southern States. A railroad also starts from the opposite side of the river, extending west as far

*as Shreveport, Louisiana. Vicksburg was the only channel ...
connecting the parts of the Confederacy divided by the
Mississippi. So long as it was held by the enemy, the free
navigation of the river was prevented. Hence its importance."[72]*

Grant made numerous attempts between January and May 1863 to
transfer his troops south of the city, but all were dismal failures. An
example was his attempt to finish a canal started in July 1862 that
would allow Union gun and transport ships to bypass the heavy guns
in Vicksburg that guarded the Mississippi. With President Lincoln's
permission, Grant ordered Major General William T. Sherman to
begin work on the previously excavated canal in January, widening
it to sixty feet with a depth of seven feet. A sudden rise in the river,
however, flooded the excavation and carried large amounts of
sediment into it. Grant attempted to save the canal by using two huge
dredges to clear out the sediment, but Rebel artillery fire from
Vicksburg caused Grant to abandon the effort by late March.

When his canal failed, Grant weighed the merit of three options
to capture Vicksburg: launch an attack on the stronghold across
the Mississippi River; attempt another approach from the north by
way of Memphis; or march his army south through Louisiana,
cross the Mississippi and approach Vicksburg from the south.
He realized a direct attack across the river would be too costly.
He was concerned that if he withdrew to Memphis, it might be seen
as a retreat that could lead to his dismissal. So, Grant decided on
his third option: march south through Louisiana.

His first attempt to cross the Mississippi and advance north
toward Vicksburg ended in defeat at Grand Gulf, Mississippi, on
April 29, 1863. However, his second attempt to turn north at Port
Gibson, Mississippi, was successful on May 1. This began a string of
victories in Mississippi at Raymond on May 12, Jackson on May 14,
Champion Hill on May 16, and Big Black River Bridge on May 17, a
total distance of about fifty miles, which cut off Vicksburg's rail

supply line to the east and brought the Union army to the outskirts of the city.

Grant sent Sherman's corps to test the defenses in front of Vicksburg on May 19. The Federals were thrown back by two divisions of Confederate infantry commanded by Lieutenant General John C. Pemberton. Following a barrage of the Rebel works by massed cannon and Union gunboats, Grant sent brigades from three corps to attack the defenses on May 22. Part of the Union force broke through the Confederate line, but they could not hold the advantage and were thrown back by Rebel defenders. When the fighting ended, Grant had sustained more than three thousand casualties to five hundred for Pemberton's troops—without gaining any appreciable ground.

Realizing that the city could not be taken by direct attack, Grant began siege operations on May 25. Union infantry blocked all access to the city from the north, south, and east. Union gunboats blocked the Mississippi River north and south of the city, and Union infantry covered the land across the river from Vicksburg.

Union gunners sent thousands of shells into the city, causing civilians and soldiers to take shelter in cellars or caves dug into the many hillsides around Vicksburg. Attempts by Confederate troops outside the city to break the siege were abandoned due to lack of adequate numbers of soldiers and resources.

Throughout June and the beginning of July, food grew scarce for the defenders, who were forced to live on pea bread (a combination of ground peas and corn meal), mules, and horses as long as supplies lasted. On July 2, Pemberton discussed his options with his commanders: attempt to break through Grant's lines or surrender. Determining that his men would not have the strength to cut through the enemy defenses, Pemberton met with Grant on July 3 to discuss terms of surrender.

True to his nickname, "Unconditional Surrender Grant," after refusing all terms earlier in the war when both Fort Henry and Fort

Donelson surrendered, Grant demanded the same from Pemberton. The Confederate general refused. That evening, Grant amended his terms to include parole. Vicksburg surrendered on July 4. Word of the fall of Vicksburg and the Union victory at Gettysburg, Pennsylvania, the previous day prompted wild celebrations throughout the North.

Port Hudson, the last Confederate stronghold on the Mississippi River, fell five days later. When he learned of the surrender, Lincoln wrote, "The Father of Waters again goes unvexed to the sea,"[73] in a letter to his close friend James Conkling.

Figure 3.3 lists the commanders, the number of troops engaged, and the number of casualties during the Vicksburg Campaign and Siege. Figure 3.4 lists the major engagements during the campaign.

FIGURE 3.3: VICKSBURG CAMPAIGN		
	Union	Confederate
Commander(s)	Major General Ulysses S. Grant	Lieutenant General John C. Pemberton
Number Engaged	77,000	48,000
Number Casualties	12,544	47,457

FIGURE 3.4: MAJOR ENGAGEMENTS DURING THE VICKSBURG CAMPAIGN			
Engagement	Date	Union Casualties	Confederate Casualties
Chickasaw Bayou	Dec 26–29	1,176	187
Arkansas Post	Jan 9–11	1,092	5,004
Port Gibson	May 1	875	787
Raymond	May 12	442	514
Jackson	May 14	286	850
Champion Hill	May 16	2,441	3,840
Big Black River	May 17	276	1,751
Siege of Vicksburg	May 18–July 4	4,835	32,697

FORT WAGNER—THE EYES OF THOUSANDS WILL LOOK ON WHAT YOU DO TONIGHT, JULY 10-18, 1863

"Now I want you to prove yourselves. The eyes of thousands will look on what you do tonight."

—The address of Colonel Robert Shaw to his regiment,
the 54th Massachusetts, before its assault on Fort Wagner[74]

The prevailing attitude in the Union army during the second year of the war was that black troops could not be trusted because they lacked the courage to fight. Even when they were officially eligible to enroll in the army after the Emancipation Proclamation, black troops were looked down on by white soldiers and officers. They were segregated in their own units, which typically were led by white officers.

A group of runaway slaves from Arkansas and Missouri unofficially formed the 1st Kansas Colored Volunteers and distinguished themselves at the Battle of Island Mounds, Missouri, on October 28, 1862. Although outnumbered by Confederates, they successfully held off several enemy attacks. This was the first recorded action of a black unit during the Civil War. It was unofficial, however, since the regiment was not enrolled in the Union army until January 13, 1863, after the Emancipation Proclamation was issued.

The members of the 1st Louisiana Engineers, another black regiment, exhibited extreme bravery during the unsuccessful attack on Port Hudson, Louisiana, on May 27, 1863. The army commander, Major General Nathaniel Banks, recognized the courage shown by this regiment that day. "Their conduct was heroic," he later wrote:

*"No troops could be more determined or more daring.…
Whatever doubt may have existed heretofore as to the efficiency*

The men of the 1st Kansas Colored Volunteers again proved their bravery on July 17, 1863, during the Battle of Honey Springs in Indian Territory, the day before another black regiment, the 54th Massachusetts Volunteer Infantry, made its ill-fated charge against Fort Wagner, South Carolina.

Recruiting for the 54th Massachusetts began in February 1863 and was completed three months later. The first black regiment raised in a Northern state (the 1st Kansas Volunteers actually was raised in Missouri, a border state during the war), the 54th trained at Camp Meigs in Readville, Massachusetts. Governor John Andrew chose twenty-five-year-old Robert Shaw, a white Bostonian who hailed from a wealthy abolitionist family, to command the regiment. It was comprised of freed blacks from across the north and included the two sons of the famous ex-slave and abolitionist speaker Frederick Douglass, as well as the grandson of former slave Sojourner Truth. Shaw enacted stringent qualifications to join the regiment, seeking only the most educated and physically fit of the recruits. The colonel also was a strict instructor and disciplinarian. By the time the regiment left Boston on June 3, 1863, it was well prepared for the action to come.

Confederate Fort Wagner, also called Battery Wagner, was located on Morris Island, which commanded the southern approach to Charleston Harbor, South Carolina. The 7th Connecticut Infantry made an unsuccessful attack on the fort on July 11, 1863. Union troops, however, were able to establish and hold a beachhead on the island to use as a base for further operations against the fort. That day came seven days later.

Roughly 1,620 men defended Fort Wagner with 15 cannon and a mortar. In preparation for the assault on July 18, Union siege guns and mortars were joined by six ironclads in the shelling of the fort for eight hours. The bomb proofs inside the fort were made of sand, however, which absorbed the effect of the shells, leaving the defenders mostly untouched and ready for the assault they knew would soon come.

The six hundred and fifty men of the 54th Massachusetts led the attack through heavy artillery and small-arms fire. Led by Shaw, a few reached the parapet of the fort and engaged in savage hand-to-hand fighting with the defenders before they were driven back. Shaw was killed during the assault—a bullet through his heart. The 54th suffered 272 casualties in the failed attempt to capture Fort Wagner.

The next day, in an act of defiance to the Union policy of white men leading black commands, a Confederate detachment stripped Shaw's body of its clothes and buried him in the sand face up with some of his men face down on top of him. When his father heard of the treatment of his son's body, he stated:

> *"Our darling son, our hero, has received at the hands of the rebels the most fitting burial possible. They buried him with his brave, devoted followers, who fell dead over him and around him. The poor, benighted wretches thought they were heaping indignities upon his dead body, but the act recoils on themselves, and proves them absolutely incapable of appreciating noble qualities. They thought to give additional pang to the bruised hearts of his friends; but we would not have him buried elsewhere if we could. If a wish of ours would do it, we would not have his body taken away from those who loved him so devotedly, with whom and for whom he gave his life."*[76]

The Confederate defenders evacuated Fort Wagner on September 6, 1863, once it was determined that any further attempt to save the fort would be futile.

By the end of the war, more than two hundred thousand blacks served in the Union army and navy. Twenty-five of these men were awarded the Congressional Medal of Honor. The first action in which a black participant warranted the medal was during the 54th Massachusetts's assault on Fort Wagner. Sergeant William Carney, the regimental color bearer, although severely wounded, held the American flag high over Fort Wagner's parapet, exclaiming, "Boys, the old flag never touched the ground."[77]

It became the subject of a popular song written by George Lothrop and Henry Mather during the late nineteenth century, "The Old Flag Never Touched the Ground."

Figure 3.5 lists the commanders, the number of troops engaged, and the number of casualties during the Battle of Fort Wagner (Battery Wagner).

FIGURE 3.5: BATTLE OF FORT WAGNER		
	Union	Confederate
Commander(s)	Brigadier General Quincy Gillmore	Colonel Robert Graham
Number Engaged	5,100	1,620
Number Casualties	1,500	222

CHICKAMAUGA—THE "ROCK OF CHICKAMAUGA" SAVES AN ARMY, SEPTEMBER 18-20, 1863

"All right, men! We can die but once! This is our time and place. Let us charge!"

—One of the last commands by Union Brigadier General William Lytle before being killed on September 20, 1863, at the Battle of Chickamauga[78]

Union Major General William Rosecrans remained in the area of Murfreesboro, Tennessee, for several months following his victory at Stones River on January 2, 1863. His opponent, General Braxton

Bragg, blocked Federal access routes to Chattanooga, Tennessee, a vital rail center on the Tennessee River. Rosecrans developed a masterful plan to maneuver around the Confederate army at the end of June, forcing it to retreat to the safety of Chattanooga.

Although forcing Bragg's army out of Tennessee was important to the Union strategy in the West, Chattanooga was Rosecrans's ultimate target. Several strategically important railroads ran through Chattanooga: the Nashville and Chattanooga, the East Tennessee and Georgia, and the Western and Atlantic. Capturing Chattanooga would cut off these important Confederate links to the West. Taking the town also would open the approach to Atlanta.

Rosecrans split his army into three columns: one north of Chattanooga, one southwest of Chattanooga into Alabama, and one near Chattanooga itself. When Bragg learned that a portion of the Union army was southwest of Chattanooga, he withdrew his army

The Battle of Chickamauga was fought in north Georgia on September 1863, and was won by General Braxton Bragg's Confederate Army of Tennessee. (Illustrated London News Ltd./Mary Evans Picture Library)

from the city on September 8 without a major battle. Concerned about how this retreat would look in the eyes of his superiors and his army (some officers were already at the point of mutiny), Bragg did not fall back to Atlanta but remained at Lafayette, Georgia, about twenty miles south of Chattanooga. He hoped to find an opportunity to strike Rosecrans's army and drive them into Tennessee. That break came sooner than Bragg expected.

Rosecrans basked in his achievement of capturing Chattanooga without a fight. Even though his army was spread out over forty miles across Tennessee and Georgia, he saw an opportunity to pursue and crush Bragg's army, which he believed was in rapid flight southeast to Atlanta.

Rosecrans ordered one of his corps to pursue the Rebel army. When the leading division of that command narrowly escaped annihilation at Davis's Cross Roads, Georgia, on September 11, the Union commander realized the precarious position of his army and ordered his scattered corps to consolidate south of Chattanooga at Lee and Gordon's Mill, Georgia. Bragg, however, had other plans.

By September 18, two Union corps were marching north along the west bank of Chickamauga Creek toward Lee and Gordon's Mill. A brief skirmish occurred between portions of both armies— and set the stage for the battle that was to begin the next morning.

Neither army knew the disposition of the opposing force. One reason was the thick forest that covered the terrain between the Lafayette Road and Chickamauga Creek. The field of vision was less than one hundred fifty yards, limiting the ability of regimental and brigade commanders on each side to control the flow of battle to their front, not knowing if they were firing on friend or enemy.

Early on September 19, a regiment of Union infantry stumbled into a regiment of Confederate cavalry that set off one of the bloodiest battles of the war. Throughout the day, both commanders engaged more and more men in the fighting as it expanded across a front several miles long, running from the road to the creek. Rebel troops would gain possession of portions of Lafayette Road, the Union lifeline, only to be driven back in bloody counterattacks. When the fighting ended due to darkness and terrain, each side was lined up roughly along the road. The Confederates had gained ground on the Yankees, but at a deadly price. By day's end, fifteen thousand Union and Confederate casualties littered the field.

After traveling more than 770 miles, using 16 trains, and taking 9 days, Confederate Lieutenant General James Longstreet and reinforcements from the Eastern Army of Northern Virginia arrived late on the night of September 19. Two of his divisions arrived a few days earlier and participated in the first day's fighting. With the arrival of Longstreet and the rest of his command, Bragg split his army into two wings, with Lieutenant General Leonidas Polk commanding the right and Longstreet the left. The Confederate commander's plan for the next morning was to attack the enemy left flank with Polk's command and then roll the attack south along the Yankee line.

Rosecrans strengthened his defenses preparing for a Confederate attack the next morning. He erected log breastworks along his line, particularly on his left flank in front of Major General George Thomas's Fourteenth Corps, which formed a salient across the Lafayette Road.

On September 20, Polk's wing of the Rebel army did not attack until 9:00 a.m., four hours later than Bragg had intended, due to poor communication of orders. For two hours, both sides fought to a draw. The Federals had their own problems with communications. A division was mistakenly ordered to pull out of line to reinforce the left flank, leaving a gaping hole on the Union right flank. The rolling Rebel attack reached that weak point in the enemy line at 11:00 a.m. Confederate troops charged through the hole, crumbled the Union right flank, and sent the enemy, all the way up to Thomas's position, fleeing to the rear. Thomas's corps, however, continued to hold what was left of the Union position.

Some Yankee officers gained quick control of their men and formed a line of defense around Snodgrass Hill, not far behind

Thomas's salient, at about 1:00 p.m. The Union position was extended south along Horseshoe Ridge with the arrival of Major General Gordon Granger's corps. Union infantry and artillery, in both positions, held off numerous charges throughout the afternoon. Finally, shortly before 5:00 p.m., Thomas was delivered an order from Rosecrans, who had fled the field for the defenses of Chattanooga earlier in the day as the right flank was swept from the field. The order was to take command of the army and coordinate the retreat of the remaining troops.

Considerable pressure was placed on the Union line once the Rebels determined that the enemy was retreating. Three regiments, the 22nd Michigan, the 21st Ohio, and the 89th Ohio, were left behind to stave off the Confederates as the rest of the army withdrew. After running out of ammunition, most of the men in the three regiments were captured.

Rosecrans had sent his chief of staff, future U.S. president Brigadier General James Garfield, to Thomas with the message to take command of the army. The Union commander was in his office in Chattanooga with two of his corps commanders, Major Generals Alexander McCook and Thomas Crittenden, both of whom had fled from the battlefield with Rosecrans, when he received a message from Garfield at the front. Over the years there has been disagreement in the content of this message. An aide to Thomas later stated that Garfield wrote, "Thomas standing like a rock. Has seven divisions intact."[79]

In the *Official Records* copy of Garfield's report, however, no mention was made comparing Thomas to a rock. Instead, Garfield wrote, "General Thomas holds nearly his old ground of this morning.... I think we may in the main retrieve our morning disaster. I never saw better fighting than our men are now doing."[80] Regardless of which message was received, all three men were happy about the fact that their army had been saved. Each of the three men must have realized, however, that, after retreating from the field with a battle still raging, their careers were permanently damaged.

No matter how hard Thomas's men fought, the battle was lost. In a 5:00 p.m. message to General-in-Chief Major General Henry Halleck, Rosecrans wrote, "We have met with a serious disaster .... Enemy overwhelmed us, drove our right, pierced our center, and scattered the troops there."[81] The next morning, he wrote President Lincoln, "We have no certainty of holding our position here [Chattanooga]."[82]

Less than a month later, Major General Ulysses S. Grant relieved Rosecrans of command. Both McCook and Crittenden also were dismissed from command and charged for the loss at Chickamauga, but were later acquitted of any guilt.

Bragg's army followed Thomas's retreating troops to the heights above Chattanooga. After the surrender of Vicksburg on July 4, 1863, and the occupation of Chattanooga without a fight, the bloody victory of Chickamauga was a much-needed boost to the Confederacy, but it would be their last significant triumph in the Western theater.

Figure 3.6 lists the commanders, the number of troops engaged, and the number of casualties during the Battle of Chickamauga.

FIGURE 3.6: BATTLE OF CHICKAMAUGA		
	Union	Confederate
Commander(s)	Major General William Rosecrans	General Braxton Bragg
Number Engaged	62,000	65,000
Number Casualties	16,170	18,454

CHATTANOOGA—THE BATTLE ABOVE THE CLOUDS, OCTOBER 28-NOVEMBER 27, 1863

"I deem it due to the cause and to myself to ask for relief from command and an investigation into the causes of the defeat."

—Confederate General Braxton Bragg in a dispatch to Adjutant General Samuel Cooper, November 29, 1863[83]

Major General Ulysses S. Grant arrived in Chattanooga on October 23, 1863, after struggling for two days over the torturous sixty-mile supply route from Bridgeport, Alabama. He had relieved Major General William Rosecrans of command of the Army of the Cumberland a week earlier and traveled to the bastion on the Tennessee River to take over the relief of the city.

Confederate General Braxton Bragg's army followed the Union army to Chattanooga after their victory at the Battle of Chickamauga, Georgia, on September 20, 1863. Without enough men to attack the defenses of the city, Bragg decided to place it under siege. He did not have enough men to completely surround the city, however, so a single road from the north remained open to Union supplies from Bridgeport, Alabama. Only twenty miles to the southeast from Chattanooga as the crow flies, it required a trip of forty miles more to avoid Rebel troops. The route was so treacherous that only food could be carried over it, but not enough to support the civilians and the Union defenders.

Soon after Grant arrived in the city, Brigadier General William "Baldy" Smith, chief engineer, described a plan to break the siege, which Grant immediately approved. Four days after Grant's arrival, Confederate troops were driven from Brown's Ferry following an amphibious assault across the Tennessee River from Chattanooga. A bridge was built across the river, and, the next day, Union troops from Bridgeport opened up a new supply line to Brown's Ferry. The "Cracker Line" was created and the siege of Chattanooga lifted. Now Grant waited for reinforcements to arrive before striking the Confederate line around the city.

The situation posed by the enemy was becoming increasingly unfavorable for Bragg in Chattanooga. But it was even worse for him within his own army. He faced a mutiny from his subordinates for failing to aggressively pursue the enemy after the victory at Chickamauga. Only six days after the victory, in a letter to Confederate Secretary of War James Seddon, Lieutenant General James Longstreet wrote:

"I am convinced that nothing but the hand of God can save us or help as long as we have our present commander [Bragg] …. Can't you send us General Lee? The army in Virginia can operate defensively, while our operations here should be offensive—until we recover Tennessee, at all events. We need some great mind as General Lee's (nothing more) to accomplish this."[84]

Instead of relieving Bragg from command, Davis ordered the reassignment of Bragg's main detractors: Lieutenant General Leonidas Polk, Lieutenant General Daniel H. Hill, and Longstreet, to other commands in the West. Not only did this reduce the size of Bragg's army, but it also removed the most capable of his field commanders.

Throughout late October and November 1863, Grant strengthened his position in Chattanooga with the addition of

Wounded Confederate soldiers arrive by train at Stevenson, Alabama, after the Battle of Chickamauga, September 1863. Engraving by American School (19th century). (Private Collection/Peter Newark Military Pictures/The Bridgeman Art Library)

about twenty thousand men under Major General William Sherman from the Army of the Tennessee and another fifteen thousand under Major General Joseph Hooker from the Army of the Potomac. Finally, Grant was ready to strike. In preparation for the main attack, Thomas's troops captured Orchard Knob at the base of Missionary Ridge on November 23, and, in the "Battle above the Clouds"[85] on November 24, Hooker's command scaled and captured Lookout Mountain.

Sherman's army crossed the Tennessee River on November 25 and attacked the Confederate right flank on the northern edge of Missionary Ridge but, after several assaults, failed to take the position. Grant had ordered Thomas's men to take the rifle pits that extended along the base of Missionary Ridge. Once that objective was carried, however, Thomas's troops did not stop as ordered, but continued up the slopes of Missionary Ridge and broke through the center of the Rebel Army of Tennessee, sending the enemy fleeing.

To protect the wagon train and artillery of his retreating army, Bragg ordered Major General Patrick Cleburne's division to hold Ringgold Gap, Georgia, about twenty miles southeast of Chattanooga, from the advancing enemy troops. The action began at about eight o'clock in the morning of November 27 and lasted for about four hours until called off by Grant. Cleburne withdrew his division soon after, having saved the Army of Tennessee's wagons and artillery.

Unlike his Union counterpart Rosecrans, Bragg did not wait to be relieved from command. On December 1, while at Dalton, Georgia, he wrote his close friend Confederate President Jefferson Davis:

> "The disaster [at Chattanooga] admits of no palliation, and is justly disparaging to me as a commander. I trust, however, you may find upon full investigation that the fault is not entirely mine... I fear we both erred in the conclusion for me to retain command here after the clamor raised against me."[86]

To the end, Bragg looked to others as the excuse for his failings. Davis replaced him with General Joseph Johnston, one of the heroes of First Bull Run.

The victory at Chattanooga was another in the string of successes for Grant. By spring 1864, he was summoned to Washington by Lincoln, promoted to Lieutenant General, and named general-in-chief of all Union armies. One of his first acts was to name Sherman as Commander of all Western Armies, setting the stage for a new type of warfare in both theaters of the war—a war of attrition that would cost many lives but ultimately lead to peace.

Figure 3.7 lists the commanders, the number of troops engaged, and the number of casualties during the actions around Chattanooga. Figure 3.8 lists major engagements during the campaign.

FIGURE 3.7: CHATTANOOGA CAMPAIGN		
	Union	Confederate
Commander(s)	Major General Ulysses S. Grant	General Braxton Bragg
Number Engaged	70,000	40,000
Number Casualties	7,839	8,739

FIGURE 3.8: MAJOR ENGAGEMENTS DURING CHATTANOOGA CAMPAIGN			
Engagement	Date	Union Casualties	Confederate Casualties
Orchard Knob	Nov 23	1,100	600
Lookout Mountain	Nov 24	408	1,251
Missionary Ridge	Nov 25	5,824	6,667
Ringgold Gap	Nov 27	507	221

TEST YOUR KNOWLEDGE ABOUT
THE MAJOR BATTLES OF 1863

1. Which Confederate general led the group of men who briefly pierced the Union line during Pickett's Charge at the Battle of Gettysburg?

    a. Lewis Armistead   b. Richard Garnett
    c. George Pickett   d. James Kemper
    e. William Lowrance

2. Vicksburg surrendered on:

    a. July 4, 1861   b. July 4, 1862
    c. July 4, 1863   d. July 4, 1864
    e. July 4, 1865

3. Which Union general failed as the commander of the Army of the Potomac at the Battle of Chancellorsville but proved a competent corps commander at Chattanooga?

    a. Ambrose Burnside   b. Joseph Hooker
    c. George McClellan   d. John Pope
    e. George Meade

4. Who was the commander of the 54th Massachusetts Volunteer Infantry?

    a. John Andrew   b. Frederick Douglass
    c. Nathaniel Banks   d. Richard Shaw
    e. Robert Shaw

5. What was the name given to the abandoned campaign, after the First Battle of Fredericksburg, that marked the end of Major General Ambrose Burnside's command of the Union Army of the Potomac?

a. The Virginia Campaign b. The River March
c. The Mud March d. The Slows
e. The Peninsular Campaign

6. Who was nicknamed the "Rock of Chickamauga"?

   a. William Rosecrans b. Gordon Granger
   c. Alexander McCook d. George Thomas
   e. Thomas Crittenden

7. Which of Thomas "Stonewall" Jackson's arms was amputated following his wounding by friendly troops?

8. Which Confederate commander achieved success at Chickamauga but failed at Chattanooga?

   a. Leonidas Polk b. Joseph Johnston
   c. Daniel Hill d. James Longstreet
   e. Braxton Bragg

9. Who did Confederate General Robert E. Lee order to attack Cemetery Hill "if practicable" at the end of the fighting on the first day of the Battle of Gettysburg?

   a. Jubal Early b. Richard Ewell
   c. John Gordon d. James Longstreet
   e. Ambrose Hill

10. Which enemy location were the Federals unable to capture during the First Battle of Fredericksburg, but finally able to overrun during the Second Battle of Fredericksburg?

   a. Salem Heights b. Slaughter Pen Heights
   c. Hampton Heights d. Marye's Heights
   e. Lee's Hill

CHAPTER FOUR

Key Battles and Campaigns of the War 1864

THE OVERLAND CAMPAIGN OF VIRGINIA—
TOTAL WARFARE, MAY 5-JUNE 24, 1864

"You see, Grant has gone into the Wilderness, crawled in, drawn up the ladder, and pulled in the hole after him, and I guess we'll have to wait till he comes out before we know just what he's up to."

> —President Lincoln's response to a Congressman
> asking why no one had heard from Grant after
> he entered the Virginia Wilderness[87]

Union Major General Ulysses S. Grant and his thirteen-year-old son, Fred, made an inauspicious entrance into Washington City by train on March 8, 1864. Grant and his son walked alone to the Willard Hotel to check in. Unimpressed by the officer standing before him, the desk clerk offered the book to check in, but when he saw "U. S. Grant and son, Galena, Illinois," his eyes widened and he had the general and boy taken to the presidential suite.

Grant was in Washington to receive an honor presented only once before. Two weeks earlier, President Lincoln had signed a bill resurrecting the rank of lieutenant general. The only other person to achieve that rank was George Washington. The main reason for giving Grant the rank of lieutenant general was so he would outrank all other generals in the army and thereby be given complete control of the war.

The strategy Grant devised for campaigning in 1864 was simple, total war. He placed Major General William T. Sherman in command of the armies in the West with the orders to put unrelenting pressure on the Confederate armies and cut a wide swath through Georgia from Chattanooga to Atlanta to the sea. In the East, Grant would accompany the Army of the Potomac, still commanded by Major General George G. Meade. His order to Meade was, "Lee's army will be your objective. Where he goes, there you will go also"[88] to hold General Robert E. Lee in check as the Union army maneuvered toward Richmond. This would not be an easy task, as evidenced by the many generals who failed before him.

The Union Army of the Potomac disappeared into the Virginia Wilderness on May 4, 1864. It was a forbidding place, as remembered by Union Brigadier General Alexander Webb, who wrote that:

> *"As for the Wilderness ... it was uneven, with woods, thickets, and ravines right and left. Tangled thickets of pine, scrub-oak, and cedar prevented our seeing the enemy, and prevented any one in command of a large force from determining accurately the position of the troops he was ordering to and fro."*[89]

Only a series of narrow roads cut through the dense underbrush. Grant wanted to gain a jump on Lee's army and pass through the Wilderness before he made contact with the enemy. Lee, on the other hand, realized that any advantage Grant would have in numbers of men and artillery would be nullified in the "tangled thickets of pine, scrub-oak, and cedar." Lee would have his wish as elements of the Union Fifth Corps struck the Rebel Second Corps in the tangle of the Wilderness on the Orange Turnpike on May 5, 1864. As fighting continued along that line, the Confederate Third Army Corps struggled with Grant's Second Corps and one division of the Sixth on the Plank Road.

The fight continued on May 6 with a Federal attack down the Plank Road, which drove the Confederates back until reinforcements under Lieutenant General James Longstreet arrived to throw the enemy line back to its original position. The fight would sputter, however, when Longstreet was wounded by his own men, reminiscent of the fate of Lieutenant General Thomas "Stonewall" Jackson. Longstreet's wound, however, did not prove fatal. Fighting along the two lines proved inconclusive throughout the day.

After years of battle experience, soldiers could sense when the battle was over. Yankees and Rebels alike expected that, as in the past, the enemy lines would break contact and retire to recover before engaging in combat again. Unlike his predecessors, however, that was not Grant's intention. At 6:30 a.m. on May 7, he issued an order to Meade: "Make all preparations during the day for a night march to take position at Spotsylvania [Court House]."[90] Unlike the many Union commanders who fell victim to Lee and his army, Grant grabbed the initiative from the Rebels and was not about to give it up. Instead of withdrawing, he slipped his army around Lee's right flank in the direction of Spotsylvania Court House, leaving behind nearly eighteen thousand Union and eleven thousand Rebel casualties.

Once Lee realized that there was no turning back for this new Union commander, he correctly concluded that Spotsylvania would be Grant's next objective, so he set sent his army southeast on a parallel course to the enemy's. The first one there would control a vital route to Richmond, and Lee had no desire to have that route fall into enemy hands.

The Fifth Corps led the Union line to Spotsylvania during the night. Its commander, Major General Gouverneur K. Warren, thought he had beaten the Confederates there until he clashed with Longstreet's corps, now led by Major General Richard Anderson, along Brock Road west of the courthouse. Warren's advance stalled. Lee won the race to Spotsylvania.

As troops on both sides arrived throughout May 8, they extended a line of breastworks, parallel to each other, on each side of Brock Road. The breastworks along a portion of the Confederate right flank formed a salient, or bulge, in front of the enemy line. Lee's engineers wanted the salient eliminated because of the danger of having the position attacked on three sides, but the Rebel commander decided to leave the line alone. The "Mule Shoe," as the salient was called, would pose a prime target for Grant's army in the days to come.

Union troops probed both flanks of the enemy line during May 9 and 10 with little effect. On the night of May 10, however, twelve Yankee regiments attacked the Mule Shoe and briefly captured a portion of the line before being repulsed by a Rebel counterattack. The brief success at the Mule Shoe set the stage for a larger assault on the position two days later.

Mistaking the movement of the Union army as a withdrawal instead of preparation to attack, Confederate artillery was removed from the Mule Shoe in the early morning of May 12. At dawn, the Union Second Corps struck that section of the enemy line and captured the position before a desperate Rebel counterattack drove the Yankees back. The fighting shifted to a section of the Confederate line now known as the "Bloody Angle," heavily protected by log breastworks six feet high, but vulnerable to attack by Union troops via a shallow valley in its front.

"The 'horseshoe' was a boiling, bubbling and hissing cauldron of death," remembered one veteran of the 93rd New York Infantry:

> *"To advance was impossible, to retreat was death, for in the great struggle that raged there, there were few merely wounded. The bullets sang like swarming bees, and their sting was death... Clubbed muskets, and bayonets were the modes of fighting for those who had used up their cartridges, and frenzy seemed to possess the yelling, demoniac hordes on either side, as soft-voiced, tender-hearted men in camp, sought, like wild beasts, to destroy their fellow men."[91]*

Intense fighting continued throughout the day without either side giving ground. Grant again attempted to capture the Mule Shoe on May 18 with the men from his Second Corps, but that attempt also failed. Finally, realizing there was nothing to gain by the continued human sacrifice at Spotsylvania, Grant began to withdraw his army around Lee's right flank, on May 20, marching south toward Guinea Station. This time, after 13 days of fighting, he left behind 18,000 casualties to the enemy's 10,000.

Lee once more anticipated Grant's movement. His army was well entrenched south of the North Anna River by the time Grant arrived. Lee had determined that the only way to defeat the numerically superior Yankee army was to remain solidly entrenched in front of it and look for any opportunity to attack and destroy any part of it. That occasion presented itself when Grant's army approached the North Anna in three lines extending several miles apart, but a shortage of experienced commanders and a bout of severe diarrhea made Lee incapable of planning and executing an effective attack. The two armies remained facing each other along the North Anna for three days before Grant once again skirted Lee's right flank, this time heading south for about thirty miles to Cold Harbor, the site of one of the battles during Union Major General George McClellan's ill-fated Peninsula Campaign two years earlier. It placed Union army within eleven miles of the Rebel capital of Richmond.

Lee realized very well that, although he had effectively shielded Richmond from the enemy, he could not continue to let Grant advance further into Virginia. "We must destroy this army of Grant's," Lee wrote to General Jubal Early, "before he gets to James River. If he gets there it will become a siege, and then it will be a mere question of time."[92] The truth of Lee's words would be proven in the months to follow.

The Union cavalry under Major General Philip Sheridan captured the strategic crossroads of Cold Harbor on May 31 and held the town in the face of heavy Rebel assault the next day. The lead elements of the rest of Grant's army arrived that afternoon and, in a late afternoon assault, had some success penetrating Lee's line before being thrown back by a Confederate counterattack.

The commander of the Army of the Potomac, Major General George G. Meade, hero of Gettysburg, was under the watchful eye of Grant. Meade proposed an attack on the Rebel right flank on

June 2, a plan that Grant approved. The Union troops picked to lead the attack were not in position on time, however, so it was postponed until June 3. This gave Lee the opportunity to fortify his seven-mile-long position, which extended from north of Bethesda Church on his left to the Chickahominy River on his right. This extra day of preparation for Lee would prove fatal to thousands of Yankees the next day.

"I have always regretted that the last assault at Cold Harbor was ever made," Grant later recorded in his memoirs. "At Cold Harbor no advantage whatever was gained to compensate for the heavy loss we sustained."[93] The Union Second, Sixth, and Thirteenth Corps attacked through a thick ground fog at 4:30 a.m. on June 3. The charge was disastrous for the Yankees. Within a half hour, the three corps suffered the majority of their casualties, and by the time the attack was officially called off, seven thousand Union soldiers lay dead or wounded between the two lines. Many of the wounded lay helplessly on the ground, suffering for four days before a truce was agreed upon. By that time, however, most had died.

Grant gained nothing from this failed attack, and the action helped to fuel accusations that he was nothing but a butcher, needlessly sacrificing his men's lives. Unlike his predecessors in the East, however, he did not retreat, lick his wounds, and engage in damage control in Washington. Grant "crawled in [the Virginia Wilderness], drawn up the ladder, and pulled in the hole after him."[94] He was determined to press forward, no matter the loss, until his job was completed.

Both armies remained in their positions until June 12, when Grant once again marched his army across Lee's right flank, this time heading to the James River. His army crossed the James on June 14, thus ending the Overland Campaign and beginning a new phase of the war in the East: the siege of Petersburg, Virginia. Lee's army was unable to stop Grant from crossing the James. The Confederate commander's worst fear—a siege—was about to begin. As he told Early several weeks earlier, the end would be a "mere question of time."[95]

Figure 4.1 lists the commanders, the number of troops engaged, and the number of casualties during the Overland Campaign. Figure 4.2 lists major engagements during campaign.

FIGURE 4.1: VIRGINIA OVERLAND CAMPAIGN		
	Union	Confederate
Commander(s)	Lieutenant General Ulysses S. Grant Major General George G. Meade	General Robert E. Lee
Number Engaged	117,000	63,000
Number Casualties	53,986	30,848

FIGURE 4.2: MAJOR ENGAGEMENTS DURING VIRGINIA OVERLAND CAMPAIGN			
Engagement	Date	Union Casualties	Confederate Casualties
Wilderness	May 5–6	18,000	10,800
Spotsylvania	May 8–21	18,000	10,000
Yellow Tavern	May 11	625	301
North Anna	May 25–26	2,623	2,517
Totopotomoy Creek	May 28–30	731	1,159
Cold Harbor	May 31–June 12	13,000	5,000
Trevilian Station	June 11–12	1,007	1,071

THE ATLANTA CAMPAIGN—JOHNSTON'S RETREAT, MAY 7-SEPTEMBER 1, 1864

"Atlanta is this great strategic point... The approaches to the Gate City—every one of them—must be made a second Thermopylae."

—Augusta Daily Constitutionalist, May 1, 1864[96]

Three days after the Union Army of the Potomac crossed the Rapidan River in Virginia to begin the Overland Campaign on May 4, 1864, Major General William T. Sherman left his supply base at Chattanooga, Tennessee, heading in the direction of Dalton, Georgia, to begin the Atlanta Campaign. When Ulysses S. Grant left the Western theater to travel to Washington to assume the rank of lieutenant general and take command of all Union armies, he left Sherman in command of the armies in the West, the Military Division of the Mississippi.

"We were as brothers," Sherman wrote of his relationship with Grant:

> *"I the older man in years, he the higher in rank. We both believed in our heart of hearts that the success of the Union cause was not necessary to the then generation of Americans, but to all future generations... Neither of us by nature was a combative man; but with honest hearts and a clear purpose to do what man could we embarked on that campaign, which I believe, in its strategy, in its logistics, in its grand and minor tactics, has added new luster to the old science of war."[97]*

Grant's strategy for spring 1864 was to pressure the Confederacy on all fronts, the two major campaigns being in Virginia and Georgia. Sherman's orders were to "move against Johnston's army [General Joseph Johnston's Army of Tennessee], to break it up and to get into the interior of the enemy's country as far as you can, inflicting all the damage you can against their war resources."[98]

Grant permitted Major General George G. Meade to remain in command of the Army of the Potomac, but he did not fully trust Meade's ability to seize the initiative from Lee and press the enemy until it had reached its breaking point. The lieutenant general, therefore, felt it necessary to oversee the campaign in the East. He did not feel the same about Sherman in the West, however. Grant had the utmost confidence in Sherman's ability. "I do not propose to lay down for you a plan of campaign," Grant wrote in his orders to Sherman, "but simply lay down the work it is desirable to have done and leave you free to execute it in your own way."[99]

Johnston's army was solidly entrenched about twenty miles southeast of Chattanooga along Rocky Face Ridge, just outside of Dalton. Sherman's troops attacked several positions along the enemy line on May 8 and 9, but they did not make any appreciable headway against the enemy. On May 11, Sherman left a portion of his command behind to demonstrate against Johnston's force while he passed around the enemy flank and marched another twenty miles south to Resaca, Georgia. When he discovered the enemy movement, Johnston hurriedly withdrew his troops to fortifications north of Resaca.

Johnston was a conservative general who preferred to remain on the defensive instead of seizing the initiative and attacking the enemy, particularly in the face of superior numbers. He felt that the preservation of his command was more important than protecting territory, so he fought a strictly defensive campaign. That would be his strategy across most of northern Georgia and ultimately would lead to his dismissal from command.

Sherman's army arrived outside of Resaca on May 13 and engaged the Rebel force the next two days, again without success. Instead of continuing the battle at Resaca, the Federals moved around the Rebel left flank, crossed the Oostanaula River, and threatened their rail supply line. Once again, Johnston withdrew his army and raced ahead of the enemy force to protect the railroad.

Instead of continuing on his direct advance on Atlanta, Sherman struck out southwest from Resaca, more than fifty miles, toward Dallas, Georgia. Anticipating his enemy's move, Johnston pursued Sherman and set up his defense at New Hope, Georgia, about four miles northeast of Dallas.

Believing that only a small portion of Johnston's command could have beaten him to New Hope, Sherman ordered his Twentieth Corps to make what turned out to be a ruinous attack on the enemy line on May 25. This was followed by another failed assault at Pickett's Mill on May 27. Brigadier General William Hazen's brigade alone suffered almost seven hundred casualties during the fight. "To how many having knowledge of the battle of the Civil War," journalist and writer Ambrose Bierce, a member of Hazen's staff (his story will be covered in Chapter 8), bitterly wrote of the half-hour fight, "does the name Pickett's Mill suggest acts of heroism and devotion performed in scenes of awful carnage to accomplish the impossible? … It is ignored by General Sherman in his memoirs, yet Sherman ordered it."[100]

In one of the few Confederate offensive actions of the campaign, a division attacked a section of the Union Army of the Tennessee's entrenched position near Dallas. The Union troops held, driving back the enemy assault.

Sherman decided to head east across Georgia to Marietta, so he once again skirted the enemy left flank and began his advance. Before the Union army could reach the city, Johnston's Confederates occupied a strong defensive position to the west at Kennesaw Mountain. Sherman marveled at the Rebels' ability to occupy strong defenses at what seemed like every turn. "The whole country is one vast fort," Sherman wrote to Grant's Chief-of-Staff Major General Henry Halleck on June 23, "and Johnston must have at least fifty miles of connected trenches with abattis and finished batteries… As fast as we gain one position the enemy has another all ready."[101]

Believing that Johnston's line was extended too long and thereby thin, Sherman decided to present a diversion on both enemy flanks and then strike the center. After an artillery bombardment by about two hundred guns, Union troops were sent forward at about 8:00 a.m. on June 27. The fight was over in less than two and a half hours. Sherman suffered heavy casualties—with little to show for them. Both armies remained in the works along Kennesaw Mountain until July 2 when Johnston first withdrew to Smyrna, Georgia. When again outflanked by Sherman, Johnston's army fell back to Peach Tree Creek, about five miles north of Atlanta.

In less than two months, Sherman had advanced through northern Georgia without a single major fight. "We had advanced into the enemy's country one hundred twenty miles," Sherman remembered:

> "with a single-track railroad, which had to bring clothing, food, ammunition, everything requisite for 100,000 men and 23,000 animals. The city of Atlanta, the gate city opening the interior of the important State of Georgia, was in sight."[102]

Sherman was not critical of his adversary, however, whom he befriended after the war. He later wrote that Johnston's army was always:

> "covered and protected by the best line of field intrenchments I have ever seen, prepared long in advance. No officer or soldier who ever served under me will question the generalship of Joseph E. Johnston. His retreats were timely, in good order, and he left nothing behind."[103]

Confederate President Davis did not share Sherman's admiration for Johnston, however. Upset that his general had surrendered so much terrain to the Federals with barely a fight, Davis considered replacing him since he shared the view expressed by the *Augusta Daily Constitutionalist* at the start of the Atlanta Campaign when it advised Johnston that: "The approaches to the Gate City—every one of them—must be made a second Thermopylae."[104] Johnston's actions during the campaign fell far short of that expectation. Unfazed by a plan Johnston proposed to attack the enemy as they crossed Peach Tree Creek, Davis replaced Johnston, naming General John Hood commander of the Confederate Army of Tennessee on July 17.

Hood had risen from cavalry captain in the Confederate army at the start of the war to corps commander by the start of the Atlanta Campaign. He had a reputation as a fearless fighter. He lost the permanent use of his left arm from a wound suffered during the Battle of Gettysburg in July 1863 and had his right leg amputated, four inches from the hip, from a wound received during the fight at

Battle of Kennesaw Mountain and the death of General Polk, from a book published in 1896. Engraving by Alfred R. Waud (1828–91). (Private Collection/The Stapleton Collection/The Bridgeman Art Library)

Chickamauga, Georgia, in September 1863. At thirty-three years of age, Hood was the youngest army commander in the Confederacy.

The news of Hood's promotion was a happy surprise for Sherman. "Hood was known to us to be a 'fighter'," Sherman wrote:

"a graduate of West Point of the class of 1853, No. 44, of which class two of my army commanders, McPherson and Schofield, were No. 1 and No. 7. The character of a leader is a large factor in the game of war, and I confess I was pleased at this change."[105]

True to his reputation, Hood wasted no time in planning his offensive. As the Union Army of the Cumberland crossed Peach Tree Creek on July 20, the Confederates massed for attack. Before he ordered his men forward, Hood learned that only two thousand five hundred men blocked a thrust Sherman was preparing to make on Atlanta. He did not launch his attack on the Union troops at Peach Tree Creek until 4:00 p.m., the delay a result of sending troops to meet Sherman's advance on Atlanta, but the enemy had already crossed the creek and was situated on high, defensible ground. For two hours, the Army of the Cumberland successfully held off the Rebel attacks. With little to show for his attempt except for five thousand casualties on the field, Hood retreated to the defenses of Atlanta

Two days later, Hood attacked Union troops east of the city to drive the enemy from an advanced position from which it could shell Atlanta. The Yankee defenders easily repulsed the disjointed Rebel attacks throughout the day. By the time Hood withdrew, he had lost almost eight and a half thousand men, more than twice as many as the enemy suffered.

Having failed in attempts to envelop Atlanta from the north and east, Sherman sent a force to the west of the city to destroy a railroad line vital to the Confederate defense of the city on July 28. Several attacks by Confederate forces were repulsed, and, at the end of the day, the Rebels suffered more than four thousand five hundred casualties to the Union's seven hundred.

Several more attempts by Sherman to cut railroad lines into Atlanta failed until August 26 when Hood discovered that the Union army had abandoned its fortifications outside the city. Rebel soldiers and citizens of Atlanta celebrated what they thought was an enemy retreat. Earlier, Hood had sent his cavalry to raid Union supply lines north of Atlanta, so his eyes on the enemy were missing. It was too late when Hood discovered that Sherman had massed his army to cut the final railroad supply lines south of the city. Union troops easily repulsed Confederate attempts to stop them on August 31 and finally captured the last railroad feeding the city at Jonesboro on September 1. That night, Hood withdrew his army from Atlanta.

Although Sherman failed in his mission to destroy the Confederate Army of Tennessee, capturing Atlanta was a major morale booster for those supporting the war in the North. "The result had a large effect on the whole country at the time," Sherman wrote:

> *"for solid and political reasons. I claim no special merit to myself, save that I believe I followed the teachings of the best masters of the 'science of war' of which I had knowledge; and, better still, I had pleased Mr. Lincoln, who wants 'success' very much. But I had not accomplished all, for Hood's army, the chief 'objective,' had escaped."*[106]

Sherman did not need to worry about Hood, however. His penchant for reckless attack soon would condemn many of his own command.

Figure 4.3 lists the commanders, the number of troops engaged, and the number of casualties during the Atlanta Campaign through Northern Georgia. Figure 4.4 lists major engagements during the campaign.

FIGURE 4.3: ATLANTA CAMPAIGN

	Union	Confederate
Commander(s)	Major General William T. Sherman	General Joseph E. Johnston General John B. Hood
Number Engaged	110,000	70,000
Number Casualties	16,779	27,637

FIGURE 4.4: MAJOR ENGAGEMENTS DURING ATLANTA CAMPAIGN

Engagement	Date	Union Casualties	Confederate Casualties
Rocky Face Ridge	May 7–13	837	600
Resaca	May 13–15	2,747	2,800
New Hope Church	May 25–26	665	350
Pickett's Mill	May 27	1,600	450
Dallas	May 28	380	1,500
Kolb's Farm	June 22	350	1,000
Kennesaw Mountain	June 27	3,000	1,000
Peachtree Creek	July 20	1,710	4,796
Atlanta	July 22	3,641	8,499
Ezra Church	July 28	700	4,642
Jonesboro	August 31–September 1	1,149	2,000

SIEGE OF PETERSBURG—LIFE IN THE TRENCHES, JUNE 15, 1864–APRIL 2, 1865

"The loss in the disaster of Saturday last foots up about 3,500, of whom 450 men were killed and 2,000 wounded. It was the saddest affair I have witnessed in the war. Such opportunity for carrying fortifications I have never seen and do not expect again to have."

—Union Lieutenant General Ulysses S. Grant in an August 1, 1864, memo to Chief-of-Staff Major General Henry Halleck concerning the failure of the Battle of the Crater[107]

On the morning of July 30, 1864, two divisions of the Union Ninth Corps anxiously waited in the darkness for a massive explosion that would destroy a portion of the Confederate entrenchments in front of Petersburg, Virginia. Coal miners in the 48th Pennsylvania Infantry began the mine on June 25. When it was completed on July 23, it was about 510 feet long and 20 feet below the Confederate line. About 8,000 pounds of dynamite were sandbagged under the Rebel works to focus the explosion upward.

While the tunnel was being dug, the Ninth Corps commander, Major General Ambrose Burnside, who had ordered the disastrous attack on the fortifications around Fredericksburg, Virginia, in December 1862 while commanding the Army of the Potomac, had a division of black troops trained to lead the assault on the breach of the enemy line caused by the explosion. Days before the scheduled action, however, Major General George G. Meade, the commander of the Army of the Potomac, ordered Burnside to choose another division to spearhead the attack. Meade was concerned that, if the attack failed and a large number of blacks were killed, it would have political repercussions throughout the North.

The explosion was set for 3:45 a.m. on July 30 so the attack could be carried out in the darkness, but there was no explosion at the set time. The sky began to brighten as the Yankee troops leading the attack impatiently waited for the eruption of earth in their front.

Four railroads from the south terminated at Petersburg, and the Richmond and Petersburg Railroad ran north to Richmond, Virginia, making Petersburg a vital supply line for the Confederate capital. If those lines were severed, Richmond would become isolated from the rest of the Confederacy. Since Union Lieutenant General Ulysses S. Grant was unable to rout General Robert E. Lee's Army of Northern Virginia and capture Richmond during the Overland Campaign, Grant decided to destroy Richmond's lifeline by capturing Petersburg.

The Yankees failed in two opportunities to capture the city in June 1864. Several lines of fortifications, with the outermost extending about ten miles, protected Petersburg. Union Major General Benjamin Butler wasted an opportunity to take the city on June 9 from only about two thousand five hundred defenders under General Pierre G. T. Beauregard, the hero of Fort Sumter and First Bull Run. From June 15–18, four Union corps attacked the Petersburg defenses, but Beauregard was gradually reinforced during those four days with troops sent by Lee and managed to hold off the Yankees' attempt to take the city. Grant suffered more than ten thousand casualties during those assaults. Unwilling to sacrifice any more men, he ordered his army to begin building fortifications across from the Rebel line. The siege of Petersburg had begun.

Grant's focus now centered on systematically capturing and destroying the remaining railroads connecting Richmond to southern supply lines: the South Side Railroad that ran from Lynchburg, Virginia; the Richmond and Petersburg Railroad; and the Weldon and Petersburg Railroad that led to Weldon, North Carolina, and extended to Wilmington, North Carolina, the only active port in the Confederacy. He sent two corps to the southwest to sever the Weldon and Petersburg Railroad on June 21, but stubborn Rebel resistance halted the Federal advance short of their target on July 23. Union troops, however, were able to extend their siege line several additional miles to the Jerusalem Plank Road.

The Union Second Corps and two divisions of cavalry crossed the James from Petersburg on July 27 to threaten Richmond as a diversion away from the explosion of the mine set for July 30. This action caused Lee to send ten thousand troops to defend the capital, leaving fewer than twenty thousand men in the trenches around Petersburg. The stage was set for what would become the Battle of the Crater.

Union troops had almost an hour to wait after the scheduled time before the explosion ripped a large hole in the Confederate defenses. The leading division, untrained in the attack since they were chosen only a short time before the charge, headed directly into a 170-foot-long, 60-foot-wide, and 30-foot-deep crater created by the explosion. The Rebels quickly recovered from the shock and began to line the top of the crater, firing small arms and artillery into the thousands of Yankees trapped in and around the basin. The Confederates blocked an advance on either side of the crater. When it came time for the Union black troops to enter the fight, they had little option but to swarm into the smoldering crevice. When the fight ended, almost four thousand Yankees were killed, wounded, or captured, compared to about one thousand five hundred Rebel casualties. The Confederates regained control of their line and forced the surviving Federals back to their original entrenchments.

For the remainder of 1864, Grant continued in his attempt to cut the rail lines into Petersburg and extend his siege fortifications to the west. Union soldiers finally captured and shut down the Weldon and Petersburg Railroad in August. Confederates still were able to receive supplies over this line by emptying the trains outside of the Union reach and transporting supplies over the Boydton Plank Road into Petersburg. With winter approaching, actions around Petersburg and Richmond reduced as each side settled into strengthening their lines and preparing for continued fighting in the spring.

As the days wore on, life in Petersburg for civilians and Confederate soldiers grew more miserable. Incessant Union shelling became a way of life. While food and other essentials continued to arrive in the city over the remaining rail line, the South Side, and over the Boydton Plank Road, the cost for these items was prohibitive to all but the wealthy. As Northern troops tightened their hold in all sections of the Confederacy, Lee's soldiers received desperate letters from home, begging them to desert to help their loved ones survive. When Abraham Lincoln was reelected President of the Union in November, all hope for a negotiated end of the war dissolved. It would be a fight to the finish, and it was only too evident to the citizens and soldiers in Petersburg that the end was drawing agonizingly closer each day.

In spring 1865, it didn't matter as much if the supply lines were open to the rest of the Confederacy. The advancing Union armies were strangling resources throughout the South. Lee's command, beset by desertion, disease, and lack of supplies, led the general to realize that, in order to survive, he had to abandon Petersburg and Richmond. He massed half of his army of sixty thousand men opposite Union Fort Stedman with the intent of breaking through the Federal line, capturing the supply depot of City Point, and joining Confederate General Joseph Johnston's force in North Carolina. He launched his attack at 4:00 a.m. on March 25, 1865. After initial success in creating a breach in the Union line, a desperate Federal counterattack plugged the hole and drove the Rebels back to their own fortifications.

Four days later, Grant seized the initiative by sending his cavalry force and two corps, under Major General Philip Sheridan, around the right flank of Lee's army to destroy the last lines of supply into Richmond and Petersburg. In a series of actions, Sheridan was successful in pushing the Confederate troops, under Major General George Pickett, to a position in front of Five Forks, Virginia, blocking Union access to the South Side Railroad. Sheridan captured Five Forks on April 1, cutting off the last supply line to Petersburg. Achieving this success, Grant ordered an assault on the city the next morning. Both sides attacked and counterattacked throughout the day. When fighting ended, the Confederates had been driven into their last line of defense in front of Petersburg.

That night, Lee ordered a withdrawal from the defenses around Petersburg and Richmond. The ten-month siege had come to an end. Lee and his army headed west along the Appomattox River, hoping to join Johnston in North Carolina. Grant was determined to stop that from happening.

Figure 4.5 lists the commanders, the number of troops engaged, and the number of casualties during the Siege of Petersburg. Figure 4.6 lists major engagements during the siege.

FIGURE 4.5: SIEGE OF PETERSBURG		
	Union	Confederate
Commander(s)	Lieutenant General Ulysses S. Grant Major General George G. Meade	General Robert E. Lee
Number Engaged	125,000	65,000
Number Casualties	45,213	27,789

FIGURE 4.6: MAJOR ENGAGEMENTS DURING SIEGE OF PETERSBURG			
Engagement	Date	Union Casualties	Confederate Casualties
Second Petersburg	June 15–18	10,600	4,700
Jerusalem Plank Road	June 21–23	2,962	572
First Deep Bottom	July 27–29	488	679
The Crater	July 30	3,798	1,491
Second Deep Bottom	August 13–20	2,900	1,300
Globe Tavern	August 18–21	4,455	1,600
Second Ream's Station	August 25	2,742	814
Chaffin's Farm	September 29–30	3,300	1,700
Peebles' Farm	September 30–October 2	2,869	1,300
Johnson's Farm	October 7	458	700
Boydton Plank Road	October 27	1,758	1,300
Second Fair Oaks	October 27–28	1,603	100
Hatcher's Run	February 5–7	1,539	1,000
Fort Stedman	March 25	1,017	2,681
Five Forks	April 1	830	3,000
Fall of Petersburg	April 2	3,894	4,852

CEDAR CREEK—SHERIDAN WILLS A VICTORY
AUGUST 7, 1864-MARCH 2, 1865

"If the enemy has left Maryland, as I suppose he has, he should have upon his heels, veterans, militiamen, men on horseback, and everything that can be got to follow to eat out Virginia clean and clear as far as they go, so that crows flying

over it for the balance of the season will have to carry their provender with them."

—Union Lieutenant General Ulysses S. Grant in a dispatch to his Chief-of-Staff Major General Henry Halleck on July 14, 1864, concerning the destruction of the Shenandoah Valley[108]

One of the elements of Lieutenant General Ulysses S. Grant's plan for total war in spring 1864 called for driving the enemy out of the breadbasket of the Confederacy, Virginia's Shenandoah Valley, and destroying the enemy's ability to continue supplying the armies in the field. To carry out this task, he put Major General Franz Sigel in command of the Department of West Virginia. Following his defeat at the Battle of New Market on May 15, 1864, however, Sigel was replaced by Major General David Hunter.

Once his army was solidly in place in the trenches before Petersburg and Richmond, Confederate General Robert E. Lee sent his Second Corps—fourteen thousand men under Lieutenant General Jubal Early—to the Valley to drive the enemy from this important region and threaten the Union capital of Washington if possible. Lee hoped to force Grant to weaken his army in front of Petersburg by sending troops to confront Early in the Valley and strengthen the defenses around Washington. Within days of assuming command, the Confederate lieutenant general won a victory at Monocacy, Maryland, on July 9, and had marched all the way up to the entrenchments protecting Washington before shelling Fort Stevens two days later. Grant hurried reinforcements to the capital and the Confederates withdrew to the Valley.

Following his victory at Kernstown, Virginia, on July 24, Early sent Confederate cavalry into Pennsylvania to demand a ransom from the citizens of Chambersburg. Refusing the Rebel demand, the city was set afire on July 30. Grant later recalled a visit he made with Hunter at the time: "I asked where the enemy was. He replied, that he didn't know."[109] Grant had enough. He telegraphed his Chief-of-Staff, Major General Henry Halleck,

"I want [Major General Philip Sheridan] put in command of all troops in the field, with instructions to put himself south of the enemy, and follow him to the death. Wherever the enemy goes, let our troops go also."[110]

In response to this telegraph to Halleck, President Lincoln offered Grant some fatherly advice:

> *"You are exactly right, but please look over the dispatches you may have received from here ever since you made that order and discover if you can that there is any idea in the head of any one here of putting our army south of the enemy or of 'following him to the death' in any direction. I repeat to you, it will neither be done nor attempted, unless you watch it every day and hour and force it."[111]*

Lincoln did not have to worry, however, for Grant had found the right man in Sheridan.

Sheridan took command of about forty-three thousand men to Early's twenty thousand. The two armies sparred for about a month in several minor engagements in the lower Shenandoah Valley north of Winchester, Virginia, before Sheridan learned from a female Union spy, Rebecca Wright, that Early had been ordered to send troops to Petersburg, which had reduced his army to less than half the size of Sheridan's. The Union general sprang his attack on Winchester on September 19. The battle began at about noon and lasted about six hours, both sides desperately holding, losing, and then counterattacking to gain back their positions. The fight turned when five Union cavalry brigades charged and overran Confederate positions along the Valley Pike, sending Rebels scurrying through Winchester and then south about twenty miles to Fisher's Hill, leaving almost four thousand casualties behind. Sheridan wired Secretary of War Edwin Stanton: "We have just sent the enemy whirling through Winchester, and are after them tomorrow."[112]

Sheridan followed up this victory two days later by seizing high ground north of Early's entrenchments along Fisher's Hill. The Union commander discovered that the enemy's line was weakest on the left flank. This was the focus of Sheridan's attack at about 4:00 p.m. the next day. It did not take long for the Confederate line to disintegrate. It ended with the Rebels fleeing south into Shenandoah's Upper Valley.

The Rebel retreat opened the Valley to Union occupation and Sheridan set out to follow his orders from Grant to destroy all resources that could support the enemy armies, including the rich farmlands of the Valley and all of its mills and barns. When his army was through, they destroyed everything for about ninety miles between Strasburg and Staunton. It took many years for the farmers of the Valley to recover from this destruction.

Confident that he had shattered Early's ability to mount any further offensive action in the Valley, Sheridan encamped his army north of Cedar Creek, south of Winchester. A brief encounter at Hupp's Hill on October 13, however, caused Sheridan to place his army on alert.

One of Early's division commanders, Major General John Gordon, and his cartographer, Captain Jedediah Hotchkiss, surveyed the Union line from Signal Knob at the tip of Massanutten Mountain and discovered several weaknesses in the enemy position, not the least of which was the lack of defenses on the left flank. The officers of the Union Eighth Corps, which held that flank, believed that the rugged nature of the terrain opposite Cedar Creek would prevent any activity on that section of the line. This proved to be a fatal error in judgment.

A local farmer alerted Early to the existence of a path along the creek and mountain that would bring his troops directly opposite the exposed enemy flank. Early, therefore, devised a three-pronged attack on the Union line spearheaded by the assault on the Eighth Corps' flank.

The attack began at 5 a.m. on October 19, easily routing the surprised Yankees. When his force scattered in the confusion of battle, the Rebel commander stopped the advance to regroup and wait to ascertain the enemy's next move.

Sheridan was absent when the enemy attacked. He had been called to Washington days earlier and did not return to Winchester until the afternoon of October 18. Having spent the night there, he learned of the attack the next morning and raced south from Winchester at 9:00 a.m. He arrived on the field at about 10:30 a.m., grabbing stragglers along the way and forcing them to return to the front. Sheridan formed a line of battle and struck back at Early at about 4:00 p.m. The Rebel line shattered when Union cavalry commanded by Major General George Custer struck their left flank. In a matter of hours, the tide had turned. It was now the Confederates who were racing from the field, leaving almost three thousand casualties behind. Sheridan lost almost six thousand men.

The result of the November election between Abraham Lincoln and the former commander of the Army of the Potomac, George B. McClellan, was up in the air until word of Sheridan's victory in the Valley and Major General William T. Sherman's success in Georgia circulated across the North. Lincoln won, ensuring that the war would continue until the Confederacy was destroyed.

Figure 4.7 lists the commanders, the number of troops engaged, and the number of casualties during the Shenandoah Valley Campaign. Figure 4.8 lists major engagements during the campaign.

FIGURE 4.7: THE SHENANDOAH VALLEY CAMPAIGN		
	Union	Confederate
Commander(s)	Major General Philip H. Sherman	Lieutenant General Jubal Early
Number Engaged	43,000	16,000
Number Casualties	11,220	7,755

FIGURE 4.8: MAJOR ENGAGEMENTS DURING SHENANDOAH VALLEY CAMPAIGN			
Engagement	Date	Union Casualties	Confederate Casualties
Third Winchester	September 19	5,020	3,610
Fisher's Hill	September 21–22	528	1,235
Cedar Creek	October 19	5,672	2,910

MARCH TO THE SEA—SHERMAN CUTS A HUGE PATH THROUGH GEORGIA NOVEMBER 15-DECEMBER 21, 1864

"Until we can repopulate Georgia it is useless to occupy it; but the utter destruction of its roads, houses, and people will cripple their military resources. By attempting to hold the roads we will lose a thousand men monthly, and will gain no result. I can make the march and make Georgia howl."

—Union Major General William T. Sherman in a letter to Lieutenant General Ulysses S. Grant requesting permission to march to the sea[113]

When Lieutenant General Ulysses S. Grant took command as general-in-chief of all Union armies, he instituted a policy of total warfare, not only against the Confederate armies, but against all their resources: factories, farms, and, as a result, civilians. Two years of war had convinced Grant that the only way to win a victory was to destroy the enemy's willingness to continue fighting, and the only way to do that was to destroy their livelihood and force them into submission.

Capturing Atlanta in September 1864 was a serious setback to the Rebel cause, but it was only one of the three objectives given to Major General William T. Sherman by Grant before beginning the Atlanta Campaign. The other two were to destroy the Confederate Army of Tennessee and to cut a deep gash into the heart of the Confederacy.

Following his withdrawal from Atlanta, General John Hood took his army into northern Georgia to disrupt the Union supply line. Sherman sent a portion of his army, about forty-five thousand men, under Major General George Thomas, the "Rock of Chickamauga," to find and destroy Hood. He then took the remainder of his army through Georgia, the heartland of the South. He was determined to hear Georgia howl by the time he reached the sea. As he told the mayor of Atlanta before launching his march, "War is cruelty, and you cannot refine it; and those who brought war into our country deserve all the curses and maledictions a people can pour out."[114]

Grant approved Sherman's plan to carry only twenty days' worth of rations when striking out on this three-hundred-mile march. Once those supplies were exhausted, his men would live off the land, seizing provisions from the farms they passed and destroying everything else in their path.

Before leaving Atlanta, Sherman ordered its evacuation before setting it on fire. The railroad terminal and as many as five thousand buildings were destroyed. Sherman admired the work of his men as they marched from the city on the morning of November 15, 1864. "Behind us lay Atlanta, smouldering and in ruins," he wrote:

> *the black smoke rising high in air, and hanging like a pall over the ruined city. Away off in the distance, on the McDonough road, was the rear of Howard's column, the gun-barrels glistening in the sun, the white-topped wagons stretching away to the south .... Some band, by accident, struck up the anthem of 'John Brown's*

About twenty-five miles northeast of Griswoldville was Milledgeville, the state capital of Georgia during the war. When Sherman's army occupied the town, they held a mock legislative session during which they voted Georgia back into the Union.

soul goes marching on;' the men caught up the strain, and never before or since have I heard the chorus of 'Glory, glory, hallelujah!' done with more spirit, or in better harmony of time and place."[115]

With Hood in northern Georgia, only about thirteen thousand Confederates, mostly young boys and old men, members of state militia units, faced Sherman's sixty thousand men during their march to the sea. The only significant attempt to stop the Federal onslaught was at Griswoldville, Georgia, on November 22. About one thousand five hundred Yankees met an equal number of enemy militia, easily driving them off after inflicting almost seven hundred casualties.

The Yankees cut a swath of devastation sixty miles wide as they marched through Georgia. They finally reached the outskirts of Savannah, Georgia, on December 12, less than a month after leaving Atlanta. Lieutenant General William Hardee defended the coastal city with fewer than ten thousand men. The Federals easily captured Fort McAllister to open a supply line with the Union fleet stationed offshore before besieging the city. Hardee rejected Sherman's demand for surrender on December 17. As the Union siege lines tightened, Hardee escaped with his men on December 20. The next day, Sherman occupied the city. "I beg to present you as a Christmas-gift," Sherman wired to President Abraham Lincoln on December 22, "the city of Savannah, with one hundred and fifty heavy guns and plenty of ammunition, also about twenty-five thousand bales of cotton."[116]

Figure 4.9 lists the commanders, the number of troops engaged, and the number of casualties during Sherman's March to the Sea. Figure 4.10 lists major engagements during the march.

FIGURE 4.9: SHERMAN'S MARCH TO THE SEA		
	Union	Confederate
Commander(s)	Major General William T. Sherman	Lieutenant General William Hardee
Number Engaged	60,000	13,000
Number Casualties	1,178	1,780

Engagement	Date	Union Casualties	Confederate Casualties
Griswoldville	November 22	62	650
Buck Head Creek	November 28	46	600
Honey Hill	November 30	746	50
Waynesborough	December 4	190	250
Fort McAllister	December 13	134	230

HOOD'S TENNESSEE CAMPAIGN—THE DESTRUCTION OF A GREAT ARMY, OCTOBER 5-DECEMBER 1, 1864

"Hood was a good man, a kind man, a philanthropic man, but he is both harmless and defenseless now. He was a poor general in the capacity of commander-in-chief. Had he been mentally qualified, his physical condition would have disqualified him.... As a soldier, he was brave, good, noble, and gallant, and fought with the ferociousness of the wounded tiger, and with the everlasting grit of the bull-dog; but as a general he was a failure in every particular."

—Confederate Soldier Sam R. Watkins[117]

John B. Hood entered the war as Colonel of the 4th Texas Infantry Regiment. He quickly rose to the command of the famous Texas Brigade and, after a fearless performance during the Battle of Antietam, was promoted to division command. As he led his men into battle on the second day at Gettysburg, Pennsylvania, in July 1863, shell fragments pierced his left hand, biceps, forearm, and elbow. He was able to save the arm, but it was paralyzed for the rest of his life.

Hood returned to command in time to participate in the Battle of Chickamauga, Georgia, a little more than two months after Gerrysburg. During the battle, he suffered his second major injury when he was wounded in the upper right leg while attempting to rally his old command, the 4th Texas. This time, Hood was not as lucky as he had been at Gettysburg. That night, his leg was amputated below his hip. Unable to keep him away from the action for long, Hood was fitted with a wooden leg and returned to command as a lieutenant general in February 1864.

Hood's stamina and determination were so strong that, even without a leg or the use of an arm, he would not resort to traveling in a wagon, but led his men on horseback. He required assistance in mounting his horse, but once in the saddle, there was little evidence of his disabilities. It is unknown if his poor performance in the battles around Atlanta or during his invasion of Tennessee was in any way due to his debilitating condition. He was an aggressive commander who, like his early mentor, Robert E. Lee, always attempted to seize the initiative. Unlike Lee, however, he was not adept in what to do once the initiative was his.

Hood surrendered Atlanta on September 1 when his last supply route into the city was cut by the Union army. He withdrew his Army of Tennessee into northern Georgia where he closely observed the actions of his adversary in Atlanta, Union Major General William T. Sherman. He planned to disrupt the Yankee supply line until he drew the enemy north from Atlanta. Failing to do that, however, he decided to carry the war back into Tennessee and drive the enemy from Nashville to draw Sherman north from Atlanta. Hood's army of thirty-five thousand men crossed the Tennessee River near Tuscumbia, Alabama, on November 16.

Sherman had sent the Army of the Cumberland under Major General George Thomas to stop Hood. Thomas sent two corps to Pulaski, Tennessee, to delay Hood until defenses could be prepared around Nashville. When Union Major General John Schofield learned that Hood had crossed the Tennessee west of Pulaski, he raced his command north to prevent the Confederates from cutting him off from Nashville. Schofield beat the enemy to

Columbia, Tennessee, crossed the swollen Duck River, and established a line of defense on high ground north of the river.

Hood circumvented Schofield's line along the Duck River and sent a portion of his command to capture a small force at Spring Hill and block Schofield's escape route. Confusion among Rebel commanders, however, prevented the Confederates from taking Spring Hill on November 29, and left open the Columbia-Franklin Pike, Schofield's escape route. The Yankees silently advanced along the road to Franklin, Tennessee, in the darkness within a few hundred yards of the unsuspecting enemy. Union Captain Levi Scofield, an engineer with the Twenty-Third Corps, recalled that during the march:

> *"we were stopped on the road by Col. George Northrup, of a Kentucky regiment of infantry. He cautioned us, 'Hist,' with finger to his lips, not to speak above a whisper, and pointed to the camp-fires on the rolling slopes within sight of the road. We could plainly see that the soldiers standing and moving about the flaring lights were Johnnies, and in the quiet of the night could hear their voices."*[118]

During the night of November 29, Hood was so confident that he had trapped Schofield that he paid little attention to warnings from a number of his subordinates that the Yankees were escaping along the pike. In the morning, when he learned of Schofield's escape, Hood chastised his commanders and ordered the army toward Franklin. The Confederate commander's fiery temper and penchant toward aggressiveness set the stage for his defeat later that day fourteen miles north at Franklin.

When Schofield arrived at Franklin later that morning, fewer than twenty miles south of Nashville, he discovered the bridge across the Big Harpeth River had been destroyed. His army occupied and strengthened previously constructed defenses south of the city with their flanks protected by the river while engineers rebuilt the bridge. It was a very formidable position with about two miles of open ground to its front, which Schofield covered by artillery.

Anxious to destroy Schofield's army before it could reach the defenses of Nashville, Hood followed the enemy to Franklin and sent eighteen brigades in a frontal assault across the open ground in front of the Yankee defenses at 4:00 p.m. without much preparation and against the advice of several of his commanders. The Confederates pierced the Union center but were thrown back by a desperate counterattack. After five hours of fighting, the number of Confederate casualties was reminiscent of the outcome of Pickett's Charge at the Battle of Gettysburg sixteen months earlier. The Confederates at Gettysburg, however, only had to charge across one mile of open ground. Hood's men advanced into heavy enemy fire for a mile more. Seven thousand three hundred Confederate casualties littered the ground in front of the Yankee works, including six generals killed or mortally wounded.

The Battle of Franklin, Tennessee, November 30, 1864. Lithograph by Louis Kurz and Alexander Allison, 1891. (Interfoto/Daniel/Mary Evans Picture Library)

Schofield withdrew from Franklin at 11:00 p.m. on November 29. By dawn the next morning, he had reached the defenses of Nashville. The ever-aggressive Hood followed closely behind.

Grant was concerned that Hood would skirt Nashville and head north. He ordered Thomas to attack immediately to prevent Hood's escape. Grant went so far as to order Thomas's removal if he did not attack. The Union general-in-chief did not have to worry, however, for Hood was not going anywhere but in front of the defenses of Nashville, searching for an opportunity to attack. Thomas seized the initiative, however, and attacked the Confederate line at 8:00 a.m. on December 15.

The Yankees struck the enemy right flank at Rains Hill first, but the bulk of the fighting throughout the day was on the Confederate left flank and continued to nightfall. Hood then withdrew his men to a position two miles south and fortified a line with his flanks on Overton's Hill and Shy's Hill. The Union attack the next day struck the Rebel works on Overton's Hill. Hood's line held for a short time, but the troops on the hill finally fled which caused the collapse of the Confederate position.

Thomas's army chased Hood south for ten days until the Confederates crossed the Tennessee River. Dejected and his army essentially destroyed, Hood resigned on January 13, 1865. The remnants of the once great Army of Tennessee would eventually join its former commander, General Joseph Johnston, in his attempt to stop Sherman's march into North Carolina.

Figure 4.11 lists the commanders, the number of troops engaged, and the number of casualties during Hood's Tennessee Campaign. Figure 4.12 lists major engagements during the campaign.

FIGURE 4.11: HOOD'S TENNESSEE CAMPAIGN		
	Union	Confederate
Commander(s)	Major General George Thomas	General John B. Hood
Number Engaged	55,000	35,000
Number Casualties	7,113	15,611

FIGURE 4.12: MAJOR ENGAGEMENTS DURING HOOD'S TENNESSEE CAMPAIGN			
Engagement	Date	Union Casualties	Confederate Casualties
Allatoona	October 5	706	897
Decatur	October 26–29	155	200
Spring Hill	November 29	350	500
Second Franklin	November 30	2,633	7,300
Second Murfreesboro	December 5–7	208	214
Nashville	December 15–16	3,061	6,500

TEST YOUR KNOWLEDGE ABOUT THE MAJOR BATTLES OF 1864

1. What was the name of Ulysses S. Grant's son, who accompanied him to Washington City in spring 1864?

   a. Tom
   b. George
   c. Fred
   d. Ambrose
   e. William

2. Which battle led to the Confederate withdrawal from Atlanta?

   a. Jonesboro
   b. Kennesaw Mountain
   c. Peachtree Creek
   d. Ezra Church
   e. Atlanta

3. How many days did the Battle of Spotsylvania Court House last?

   a. 10
   b. 13
   c. 14
   d. 16
   e. 18

4. Which Confederate defeat led to the Union capture of the South Side Railroad, the last supply line into the Rebel stronghold of Petersburg?

   a. Globe Tavern   b. Five Forks
   c. Hatcher's Run   d. Ream's Station
   e. Fair Oak

5. How many Confederate generals were killed or mortally wounded at the Battle of Franklin?

   a. 2   b. 3
   c. 4   d. 5
   e. 6

6. How many days did the Battle of the Wilderness last?

   a. 1   b. 2
   c. 3   d. 4
   e. 5

7. The Battle of the Crater took place during the siege of:

   a. Chattanooga   b. Atlanta
   c. Vicksburg   d. Petersburg
   e. Nashville

8. How wide was the Yankee swath of devastation through Georgia?

   a. 10 miles wide   b. 20 miles wide
   c. 40 miles wide   d. 60 miles wide
   e. 80 miles wide

9. Put these three battles in the order in which they were fought during the Shenandoah Valley Campaign:

   a. Third Winchester   b. Fisher's Hill
   c. Cedar Creek

10. Which Union attack during his Virginia Overland Campaign did Grant later state he regretted making?

a. Wilderness
b. Spotsylvania
c. North Anna
d. Cold Harbor
e. Yellow Tavern

Extra Credit for the True Civil War Buff: Place the Following Battles and Campaigns in Chronological Order

a. Chattanooga
b. Gettysburg
c. Second Bull Run
d. Atlanta Campaign
e. Siege of Vicksburg
f. First Bull Run
g. Hood's Tennessee Campaign
h. Antietam
i. *Monitor* vs. *Virginia*
j. Overland Campaign
k. Shiloh
l. Cedar Creek
m. Chickamauga
n. Seven Days
o. Fredericksburg
p. Chancellorsville
q. Stones River
r. March to the Sea
s. Siege of Petersburg
t. Fort Wagner

CHAPTER FIVE

Peace at Last

"We meet this evening not in sorrow, but in gladness of heart. The evacuation of Petersburg and Richmond, and the surrender of the principal insurgent army [Robert E. Lee's Army of Northern Virginia], give hope of a righteous and speedy peace, whose joyous expression cannot be restrained. In the midst of this, however, He from whom blessings flow must not be forgotten."

—Abraham Lincoln's opening words during his last public address given from the White House balcony on April 11, 1865, three days before his assassination[119]

APPOMATTOX COURT HOUSE, VIRGINIA—
AN AFFECTIONATE FAREWELL
APRIL 9, 1865

"What General Lee's feelings were I do not know. As he was a man of much dignity, with an impassible face, it was impossible to say whether he felt inwardly glad that the end had finally come, or felt sad over the result, and was too manly to show it."

—Union Lieutenant General Ulysses S. Grant's observation of Robert E. Lee at the ceremony[120]

Four figures on horseback passed through the Confederate lines near Appomattox Court House, Virginia, in the early afternoon of April 9, 1865. They rode across the no-man's-land between the two armies toward the quiet village along the Richmond-Lynchburg Stage Road. There was no sense of urgency in their horses' gait. Accompanied by his military secretary, Colonel Charles Marshall, Union Lieutenant General Ulysses S. Grant's aide-de-camp, Union Lieutenant Colonel Orville Babcock, and an orderly, Confederate General Robert E. Lee, on the longest ride of his military career, was about to surrender his Army of Northern Virginia.

Following his withdrawal from Petersburg and Richmond, on April 2, 1865, Lee led his army west through southern Virginia in the hope of resupplying his troops at Lynchburg before heading south to unite with General Joseph E. Johnston's army in North Carolina. He was closely pursued by the Union Army of the Potomac, which remained south of the Rebels to block any attempt to join Johnston.

For seven days, the two armies fought a series of skirmishes and minor engagements, the largest being near Sailor's Creek, Virginia, on the evening of April 6. The action was actually three separate fights: one at the Lockett farm, another at the Hillsman farm, and the third between the Marshall and Harper farms. All three had the same result with Union forces routing the Confederates at each location. When the fighting ended, Yankee troops captured thousands of enemy soldiers, including eight generals, and more than two hundred supply wagons. When Lee saw his fleeing troops, he exclaimed, "My God! Has the army dissolved?"[121]

It was not until the morning of April 9 that Lee finally realized that his attempt to prolong the war was hopeless. His supplies at Lynchburg were blocked by the enemy, and he was virtually surrounded by Grant's command. He told his aides, "Then there

The surrender of Lee. (American Antiquarian Society, Worcester, Massachusetts, USA/The Bridgeman Art Library)

is nothing left me but to go and see General Grant, and I would rather die a thousand deaths."[122]

Since April 7, Lee had been engaged in correspondence with Grant regarding possible surrender. His correspondence to the Union general on the morning of April 9 led Grant to give Lee the choice of deciding the site of their meeting to discuss terms of surrender. As Lee and his party of three entered Appomattox Court House, they met Wilbur McLean, who led them to his home. Lee waited inside about a half hour before Grant arrived at 2 p.m.

The two men spoke briefly about their first and only prior meeting during the Mexican War in 1846 before getting down to the issue of surrender. Lee knew of Grant's nickname "Unconditional Surrender" Grant, earned for the terms he had extended after his capture of Forts Henry and Donelson, Tennessee, in February 1862, and Vicksburg, Mississippi, in July 1863. Grant, realizing this was the first step toward reconciliation of the two nations and that there were still more than one hundred fifty thousand Rebel troops in the Western theater who had not yet surrendered, was generous in his terms to Lee, allowing all officers to keep their side arms, private horses, and baggage. Grateful for Grant's generous terms, Lee signed the surrender document. Grant also directed that rations be issued to Lee's twenty-eight thousand men, many of whom were starving.

He remained in Grant's company for more than an hour before returning to his lines. One of his soldiers later recalled his ride through the Confederate camp:

"When, after his interview with Grant, General Lee again appeared, a shout of welcome instinctively ran through the army. But instantly recollecting the sad occasion that brought him before them, their shouts sank into silence, every hat was raised, and the bronzed faces of the thousands of grim warriors

bathed with tears. As he rode slowly along the lines hundreds of his devoted veterans pressed around the noble chief, trying to take his hand, touch his person, or even lay a hand upon his horse, thus exhibiting for him their great affection. The general then, with head bare and tears flowing freely down his manly cheeks, bade adieu to the army. In a few words he told the brave men who had been so true in arms to return to their homes and become worthy citizens."[123]

Lee expressed his love for his men in the last sentence of his farewell message to them:

"With an unceasing admiration of your constancy and devotion to your Country, and a grateful remembrance of your kind and generous consideration for myself, I bid you all an affectionate farewell."[124]

DURHAM, NORTH CAROLINA— WITH FEELINGS OF CORDIAL FRIENDSHIP APRIL 26, 1865

"Hardee [Lieutenant General William Hardee] ... reported the Salkehatchie swamps as absolutely impassable; but when I heard that Sherman had not only started, but was marching through those very swamps at the rate of thirteen miles a day, making corduroy road every foot of the way, I made up my mind there had been no such army since the days of Julius Caesar."

—Confederate General Joseph E. Johnston recalling
his thoughts about the might of Major General
William T. Sherman's army[125]

On April 17, 1865, a detachment of Confederate cavalry rode east from Hillsborough, North Carolina, toward the state capital at

Raleigh. In the detachment was General Joseph E. Johnston. The purpose of the trip was to meet Union General William T. Sherman to discuss terms for the Confederate surrender. Richmond, Virginia, had fallen fifteen days before, followed seven days later by the surrender of General Robert E. Lee's Army of Northern Virginia to Lieutenant General Ulysses S. Grant. The prospects were bleak for Johnston to continue his fight. Not only did he face Sherman's battle-hardened veterans to the east, but now that Lee surrendered, the Union Army of the Potomac threatened from the north.

On February 23, 1865, Johnston had been placed in command of the Department of South Carolina, Georgia, and Florida and the Department of North Carolina and Southern Virginia by Lee, who was then the newly appointed general-in-chief of the Confederate armies. Johnston assumed his new command just as Sherman's army was about to enter North Carolina after cutting its deep swath through Georgia and South Carolina.

Realizing that his starving and ragged men were no match for Sherman's superior army, Johnston decided to attack an isolated section of the enemy. He was able to drive back a portion of the Yankee command in the Battle of Bentonville on March 19, 1865, but was himself driven back once Union reinforcements arrived. The Confederates withdrew about one hundred thirty miles to Greensboro, preparing for a last stand.

Johnston met with Confederate President Jefferson Davis, who was himself eluding a Union pursuit following his escape from Richmond, to discuss possible surrender. Receiving his President's approval, Johnston sent a courier to Sherman on April 14 asking for a truce and a meeting to discuss terms of surrender.

The opposing generals first met on the Hillsborough Road just west of Durham Station, halfway between their lines. They proceeded to the farm of James Bennett to discuss surrender.

When Sherman suggested they sign the same terms that Lee had earlier signed with Grant, Johnston refused. During their meeting a few days earlier, Johnston and Davis discussed asking for terms that would map a permanent peace throughout the South rather than just the surrender of an army. Sherman agreed to meet the next day, April 18, to continue this discussion. The Union general was anxious to gain agreement on the demobilization of the Confederate armies before they could break up into guerrilla bands, "roaming through the South, keeping the country in a disturbed condition for months, and perhaps for years."[126]

The next day, the two men agreed to a broad, conditional treaty for peace. It called for all Confederate armies to immediately disband, the recognition of present Southern state governments whose members were willing to take an oath of allegiance, the reinstatement of Federal courts throughout the South, and the reinstatement of civil and political rights "as long as they live in peace."[127]

Jefferson Davis accepted the terms of surrender, but Union President Andrew Johnson rejected the treaty due to its liberal terms. Grant forwarded word of the rejection to Sherman on April 21, ending his letter with, "Please notify General Johnston, immediately on receipt of this, of the termination of the truce, and resume hostilities against his army at the earliest moment you can."[128]

Johnston and Sherman met a third time at the Bennett farm on April 26 and signed terms of surrender similar to that signed by Lee seventeen days earlier. Once the terms of surrender were signed, Sherman's men distributed ten days' worth of rations to Johnston's famished army of more than thirty-five thousand men.

Just as Lee had expressed his devotion to his troops in his final address, Johnston ended his last message to his troops on a similar note, saying:

"I shall always remember with pride the loyal support and the generous confidence you have given me. I now part with you with deep regret, and bid you farewell with feelings of cordial friendship and the earnest wishes that you may have hereafter all the prosperity and happiness to be found in the world."[129]

The April 26 surrender at Bennett's Farm was not the last time Johnston and Sherman were to meet. They struck a friendship that carried into the postwar years. Johnston was a pallbearer at Sherman's funeral on February 19, 1891. The day was very cold and rainy, but Johnston walked in the procession, through the streets of New York, without his hat as a sign of respect for his fallen dear friend and one-time enemy. Johnston caught pneumonia shortly after the funeral and died several weeks later.

IRWINSVILLE, GEORGIA—
CAPTURED IN WOMEN'S CLOTHES
MAY 10, 1865

"One Hundred thousand dollars' reward will be paid to any person or persons who will apprehend and deliver Jefferson Davis to any of the military authorities of the United States. Several million dollars of specie reported to be with him will become the property of the captors."

—Order from Major General James H. Wilson
dated April 28, 1865[130]

At about 3:30 a.m. on May 10, 1865, a detachment of about one hundred thirty men of the 4th Michigan Volunteer Cavalry attacked a sparsely guarded camp near Irwinsville, Georgia. Inside one of the tents was Confederate President Jefferson Davis, who had been eluding pursuing Union troops since escaping from Richmond, Virginia, on April 2. At first he thought that the men attacking his camp were ex-Confederate marauders who had been pursuing the Davis party for several days, but when he saw the blue coats, he knew it was Federal cavalry.

Davis had been traveling with his wife and children for the previous five days. Prior to that time, he had traveled with a party of cavalry in an attempt to escape to Texas with the intent of reestablishing the Confederate government. His wife and children had been heading into the deep South on their own, under guard, since fleeing Richmond. Concerned for their safety, however, Davis returned to protect them while they traveled through this land turned squalid by four years of war.

Jefferson Davis, American statesman and President of the Southern Confederacy. (Mary Evans Picture Library)

Concerned for her husband's safety as the Union cavalry rushed their camp, she urged him to flee. As Davis left the tent, he grabbed his wife's overcoat by mistake, and she threw a shawl over his head to attempt to hide his identity. Davis later wrote in his memoir that:

"I had gone perhaps fifteen or twenty yards ... when a trooper galloped up and ordered me to halt and surrender, to which I gave a defiant answer, and, dropping the shawl and raglan from my shoulders, advanced toward him; he leveled his carbine at me, but I expected, if he fired, he would miss me, and my intention was in that event to put my hand under his foot, tumble him off on the other side, spring into his saddle,

Following his declaration that the war had ended, President Andrew Johnson called for a review of Union armies through the streets of Washington City, to receive tribute for their victory, much as the Roman troops experienced through the streets of Rome following successful conquests almost two thousand years earlier. Johnson also hoped that a celebration of victory would improve the mood in the nation's capital following the assassination of Abraham Lincoln less than a month earlier.

It took more than six hours for the eighty thousand men of the Eastern Army of the Potomac to pass in review on May 23 before the citizens of Washington, including the President, his Cabinet, General-in-Chief Ulysses S. Grant, and many other dignitaries. It took another six hours the next day for the sixty-five thousand men of the Western Armies of Georgia and Tennessee to pass.

and attempt to escape. My wife, who had been watching, when she saw the soldier aim his carbine at me, ran forward and threw her arms around me. Success depended on instantaneous action, and, recognizing that the opportunity had been lost, I turned back, and, the morning being damp and chilly, passed on to a fire beyond the tent."[131]

Word had been circulating that Davis had escaped Richmond with millions of dollars in gold coins. Yankee cavalrymen, looking for this bounty, tore through the wagons, scattering the items across the camp. No treasure was found.

Davis was treated as poorly as his baggage. One Union soldier approached him saying, "Well, Jeffy, how do you feel now?"[132] The soldier was scolded by an officer and ordered to treat the Confederate President with respect.

The Grand Review of the Army of the Potomac before President Johnson at Washington, June 17, 1865. (Photo © Liszt Collection/The Bridgeman Art Library)

Although he had been captured in his wife's overcoat and shawl, reports circulated that Davis had been captured in one of his wife's dresses. This was only one of many humiliations the former Confederate President would face in the years to come. Unrepentant to the end, Davis stated in an address to veterans of the Army of Tennessee in 1878, eleven years before his death, that:

> *"Without desire for a political future, only anxious for the supremacy of the truths on which the Union was founded, and which I believe to be essential to the prosperity and the liberties of the people, it is little to assume that I shall die, as I have lived, firm in the State rights faith."*[133]

TEST YOUR KNOWLEDGE ABOUT THE WAR'S END

1. Which Virginia town was the Confederate Army of Northern Virginia hoping to reach for resupplies after the fall of Richmond?

   a. Appomattox Station b. Winchester
   c. Lynchburg   d. Roanoke
   e. City Point

2. Who was General Robert E. Lee's secretary?

   a. Colonel Orville Babcock
   b. Colonel Jedediah Hotchkiss
   c. Colonel Samuel Carroll
   d. Colonel Thomas Coyne
   e. Colonel Charles Marshall

3. Put these events in chronological order:

   a. Surrender of Jefferson Davis
   b. Fall of Richmond
   c. Surrender of Robert E. Lee
   d. Surrender of Vicksburg
   e. Surrender of Fort Donelson

4. On whose farm did the surrender of Robert E. Lee's army take place?

   a. Lockett Farm
   b. Marshall Farm
   c. Bennett Farm
   d. McLean Farm
   e. Harper Farm

5. On whose farm did the surrender of Joseph Johnston's army take place?

   a. Lockett Farm
   b. Marshall Farm
   c. Bennett Farm
   d. McLean Farm
   e. Harper Farm

6. Which battle was the last fought by Johnston's army?

   a. Sailor's Creek
   b. Appomattox
   c. Bentonville
   d. Raleigh
   e. Five Forks

7. Which battle was the last fought by Lee's army?

   a. Sailor's Creek
   b. Appomattox
   c. Bentonville
   d. Raleigh
   e. Five Forks

8. How many hours did it take the Union Army of the Potomac to pass through the streets of Washington during the Grand Review in Washington?

   a. 2 hours
   b. 4 hours
   c. 5 hours
   d. 6 hours
   e. 8 hours

9. Did the Eastern or Western armies parade first through the streets of Washington during the Grand Review?

   a. Eastern
   b. Western

10. Lincoln was assassinated how many days after Lee's surrender?

   a. 1
   b. 3
   c. 5
   d. 7
   e. 9

CHAPTER SIX

Four Years of War— The Numbers

"There is many a boy here who looks on war as all glory, but, boys, it is all hell. You can bear this warning voice to generations yet to come."

—Major General William T. Sherman in a postwar address to members of the Grand Army of the Republic[134]

THOSE WHO SERVED—NORTH AND SOUTH

"The actual soldier of 1861–'65, North and South, with all his ways, his incredible dauntlessness, habits, practices, tastes, language, his fierce friendship, his appetite, rankness, his superb strength and animality, lawless gait, and a hundred unnamed lights and shades of camp, I say, will never be written—perhaps must not and should not be."

—Walt Whitman[135]

The North held a definite advantage over the South in population and the number of men eligible for military service when the war began, as shown in Figure 6.1. While the border states made a significant contribution to the Confederate armies, it didn't come close to making up for the Northern states' superiority in numbers. As the South's ability to fill openings in its military ranks became more difficult with each passing year, elderly men in their fifties and beyond and young boys in their early teens were pressed into service. The Confederate legislature even passed a declaration to press slaves into military service, but the war ended before any armed slaves reached the front lines.

FIGURE 6.1: 1860 CENSUS			
	Free	Slaves	Military Age*
Northern States and Territories	18,669,737	46	4,559,872
Border States	2,779,455	432,586	583,685
Southern States	5,482,222	3,521,150	1,064,193
Totals	26,931,414	3,953,782	6,207,750
* includes nonslaves			

The Northern War Department kept accurate records of the number of men who served, were wounded, died in battle, and succumbed to disease. As accurate as the statistics are for the Union army, the figures for the Confederacy are purely estimates.

Much of the information that was recorded in the field and submitted to Confederate state and national governments was destroyed prior to the Union armies' occupation of state capitals and the Confederacy's capital in Richmond, Virginia.

Figure 6.2 details some of the significant numbers for those who served and lost their lives during the war. All figures relating to Confederate enrollment in the army or casualties are mere speculation based on approximations using records that survived the war.

FIGURE 6.2: STATISTICS FROM THE WAR [136]		
	Union	Confederate
Total served in the war	2,778,304	1,234,000
Total killed in battle	67,058	52,954
Total died of wounds	43,012	21,570
Total died of disease	199,720	59,297
Total died in prison	24,866	26,436
Total other deaths	24,872	*
Total wounded (survived)	268,530	194,026
Total desertions	125,000	104,428
* = information not available		

In most categories, Confederate estimates are likely significantly lower than the actual numbers would be, particularly in the number of soldiers who died from disease. A soldier on either side was more likely to succumb to disease than die from a wound suffered in battle, particularly during the first few years of the war. When soldiers from rural areas camped in unsanitary conditions with men from the cities, they often became victims of diseases they had never been exposed to before. Disease quickly spread through the ranks, fueled by a lack of natural immunity, at times effecting whole companies and even regiments. Prior to the Battle of Antietam, the 4th Ohio Volunteer Infantry was temporarily detached from its brigade because the majority of its men were suffering from the measles. This situation was not uncommon in Northern or Southern ranks.

Much has been written about the Confederate prison of Andersonville and the horrible conditions under which the Union prisoners were forced to live, but, as shown in Figure 6.2, more Confederate than Union prisoners died during the war. Once Northern authorities learned about the conditions in Rebel prison camps, the situation worsened for some Confederate prisoners throughout the North. (A further description of prisoner of war camps on both sides will be covered in Chapter Seven.)

As the war progressed, food, clothing, and other essentials became scarce throughout the South, for civilians and soldiers alike. Desperate pleas for help from family members caused the desertion rate from the Confederate Army to begin to increase dramatically in 1863 and 1864. One of the major reasons for the spike in Union desertions was precipitated by the bounty or bonus system instituted as part of Federal draft laws. Soldiers were paid substantial bounties, if they enlisted, by both the national and state governments. Draftees were able to avoid service if they provided a substitute, whom they often paid for. Many Union soldiers collected their bounties or their fees for acting as a substitute before deserting and reenlisting for more bounty or substitute pay.

BATTLES AND SKIRMISHES—THE NUMBERS

"Skirmish! hell and damnation! I'd like to know what he calls a battle."

—Confederate Major General Leonidas Polk, an Episcopal Bishop, when informed that his adversary, Brigadier General Ulysses S. Grant, called their engagement at Belmont, Missouri, on November 7, 1861, a skirmish[137]

FIGURE 6.3: NUMBER OF MAJOR BATTLES AND ENGAGEMENTS IN EACH STATE [138]

	1861	1862	1863	1864	1865	Total
Alabama	-	10	12	32	24	78
Arizona	-	1	1	1	1	4
Arkansas	1	42	40	78	6	167
California	-	1	4	1	-	6
Colorado	-	-	-	4	-	4
Dakota	-	2	5	4	-	11
District of Columbia	-	-	-	1	-	1
Florida	3	3	4	17	5	32
Georgia	-	2	8	92	6	108
Idaho	-	-	1	-	-	1
Illinois	-	-	-	1	-	1
Indian Territory	-	2	9	3	3	17
Indiana	-	-	4	-	-	4
Kansas	-	-	2	5	-	7
Kentucky	14	59	30	31	4	138
Louisiana	1	11	54	50	2	118
Maryland	3	9	10	8	-	30
Minnesota	-	5	1	-	-	6
Mississippi	-	42	76	67	1	186
Missouri	65	95	43	41	-	244
Nebraska	-	-	2	-	-	2
Nevada	-	-	-	2	-	2
New Mexico	3	5	7	4	-	19
New York	-	-	1	-	-	1
North Carolina	2	27	18	10	28	85
Ohio	-	-	3	-	-	3
Oregon	-	-	-	3	1	4
Pennsylvania	-	-	8	1	-	9
South Carolina	2	10	17	9	22	60
Tennessee	2	82	124	89	1	298
Texas	1	2	8	1	2	14
Utah	-	-	1	-	-	1
Virginia	30	40	116	205	28	419
Washington Territory	-	-	1	-	-	1
West Virginia	29	114	17	19	1	180
Totals	156	564	627	779	135	2,261

There were more than ten thousand five hundred armed engagements during the Civil War, ranging from battles to minor skirmishes. Many of these were small affairs that a researcher could discover only after thoroughly studying *The War of the Rebellion: A Compilation of the Official Records of the Union and Confederate Armies,* which is the 128-volume collection of all after-battle reports and correspondence of both sides during the war. Figure 6.3 lists the states in which more than two thousand of those major battles and engagements took place. Virginia was the site of the greatest number followed by Tennessee, Missouri, and Mississippi.

Although the war was fought primarily within the boundaries of Confederate and Border States, New York, Illinois, Ohio, Idaho, Utah, and several other Union states and territories did not escape the conflict.

FAMOUS REGIMENTS—HEROICS AND LOSS

"The regiment is the family. The colonel, as the father, should have a personal acquaintance with every officer and man, and should instill a feeling of pride and affection for himself, so that officers and men naturally look to him for personal advice and instruction. In war the regiment should never be subdivided, but should always be maintained entire. In peace this is impossible."

—William T. Sherman[139]

The regiment was the basic fighting unit employed during the war and the backbone of the armies on both sides. Several regiments formed brigades and entered battles together as members of that larger unit. Once a regiment gained a reputation as an effective fighting unit, it often was singled out during critical moments in a battle to perform special deeds, such as plugging a hole in a line, sacrificing its members to blunt an attack of a larger enemy body of soldiers, or leading assaults on impregnable enemy positions.

Members of volunteer regiments often were recruited from the same town or section of the county or state. These men were related, grew up together, or worked with each other in their civilian lives. They trained together from the beginning of their service and elected their company and regimental officers. When in a fight, they looked out for each other and carried out their assignment knowing the impact of failure on those they loved and admired.

Figure 6.4 lists those regiments on both sides that were called on to perform critical deeds in a given battle and experienced heavy losses as a consequence of their heroics.

The 1st Minnesota entered the Battle of Gettysburg with 262 men ready for battle. When a Confederate brigade broke through the

FIGURE 6.4: GREATEST PERCENTAGE OF REGIMENTAL LOSS IN BATTLE [140]

UNION		
Regiment	Battle	% Loss
1st Minnesota	Gettysburg	82
141st Pennsylvania	Gettysburg	76
101st New York	2nd Bull Run	74
25th Massachusetts	Cold Harbor	70
36th Wisconsin	Bethesda Church	69
20th Massachusetts	Fredericksburg	68
8th Vermont	Cedar Creek	68
81st Pennsylvania	Fredericksburg	67
CONFEDERATE		
Regiment	Battle	% Loss
3rd North Carolina	Antietam	90
23rd North Carolina	Gettysburg	87
1st Texas	Antietam	82
21st Georgia	2nd Bull Run	76
26th North Carolina	Gettysburg	72
6th Mississippi	Shiloh	71
8th Tennessee	Stones River	68
South Carolina Palmetto Sharpshooters	Glendale	68

Union line along the Emmitsburg Road on the second day of fighting and threatened a critical Yankee position on the battlefield, the men of the 1st Minnesota were called on to charge the enemy to blunt the attack. By the time the fighting ended, 215 members of the regiment, 82 percent, were either killed or wounded.

On the Confederate side, the 3rd North Carolina had a higher percentage of losses during the Battle of Antietam than any other Southern unit in all other battles of the war. The 3rd North Carolina well earned this distinction during the battle. Colonel William De Rosset was in command of the regiment and the 4th Georgia during the Battle of Antietam. He later recounted that:

"I carried into action ... the morning of the 17th of September, 520 men, and the loss on that and the following day was 330 men, and 23 out of 27 officers, of which latter 7 were killed or died from their wounds within a few days. Most of the loss was sustained in less than two hours of fighting on the first day. We were in position near the 'East Wood,' having gone into action through the yard of the Mumma house (which was set fire to by my orders), and for an hour were fighting three lines of Federals, when a division, in column of battalion, came up, and, halting within one hundred yards of my right company, the right of the brigade, opened fire, enfilading my command and causing the heavy loss sustained in so short a time."[141]

Of the sixteen regiments listed in Figure 6.4, only two reflect losses in battles in the Western theater. If the list of Union percentage of loss in a single battle was increased from the highest eight to the highest fifty incidents, only seven occurred in battles in the Western theater, and three of those losses were during the Battle of Chickamauga. Twenty-two, or almost half, occurred during the battles of Gettysburg or Antietam. Does this fact mean that the battles in the Eastern theater were more violent or larger engagements? More fighting occurred in the West than in the East during each year of the war. On the other hand, Figure 6.5 shows that the engagements in the East involved many more men than those in the West:

FIGURE 6.5: NUMBER OF MEN ENGAGED IN BATTLES*					
Theater	1861	1862	1863	1864	Total
Eastern	36,982	412,027	265,800	355,869	1,070,678
Western	0	75,784	342,972	270,523	689,279
Total	36,982	487,811	608,772	626,392	1,759,957
* battles covered in this book					

The actual number of men engaged, shown in Figure 6.5, does not necessarily answer the question of why the percentage of loss was generally larger in the East than West. There is no easy answer for that question other than to note that the strategies and tactics were different in the West than in the East. The war in the West was a series of campaigns made of a number of battles fought sometimes days apart in different locations. In the East, however, campaigns of many battles gave way, particularly during the first two years of the war, to single battles where everything was at stake. This strategic and tactical approach to battle created a do-or-die mentality that did not necessarily exist in the West.

DEATH IN THE RANKS— COMMANDERS AND GENERALS

"As the bullets whistled by, some of the men dodged. The general said laughingly, 'What! What! Me, dodging this way for single bullet! What will you do when they open fire along the whole line? I am ashamed of you. They couldn't hit an elephant at this distance.' ... The general touched him gently with his foot, and said, 'Why, my man, I am ashamed of you, dodging that way,' and repeated the remark, 'They couldn't hit an elephant at this distance.' For a third time the same shrill whistle, closing with a dull heavy stroke, interrupted our talk, when, as I was about to

resume, the general's face turned slowly to me, the blood spurting from his left cheek under the eye in a steady stream."

—Union Sixth Corp Chief-of-Staff Martin McMahon on the moments before Major General John Sedgwick's death by the hand of a Confederate sniper at Spotsylvania Court House[142]

When in battle, the commander of a Union or Confederate army was dependent on his subordinate commanders to carry out a plan of battle. The levels of command and their responsibilities in battle included those listed in Figure 6.6.

The official rank of men who served as army, corps, and division commanders in the Union forces was usually major general. In the Confederacy, army commanders were generals, corps commanders were lieutenant generals, and division commanders were major generals. When required, men of lesser rank took command of divisions and brigades.

Army, corps, and division commanders generally were stationed well behind the battle line, but situations arose during which their presence was required at the front, leading to many of the deaths shown in Figure 6.7. With the advent of rifled muskets and artillery, even walking, standing, or riding a horse well behind the lines proved fatal for some commanding generals.

FIGURE 6.6: ROLES OF COMMANDERS IN BATTLE		
Level of Command	Position in Battle	Responsibility in Battle
Army Commander	Army HQ	Set strategic objections and give general orders before start of battle
Corps Commander	Corp HQ	Coordinate infantry divisions and artillery
Division Commander	Div HQ	Set tactical direction of division
Brigade Commander	Battle Line	Set tactical direction of brigade
Regimental Commander	Battle Line	Set tactical direction of regiment
Company Commander	Battle Line	Set tactical direction of company

FIGURE 6.7: HIGHER RANKING GENERALS KILLED IN BATTLE [143]

UNION

Name	Command	Battle	Manner of Death
Major General James McPherson	Army of Tennessee	Atlanta (1864)	Riding between lines
Major General Joseph Mansfield	12th Corps	Antietam (1862)	Riding along battle line
Major General John Reynolds	1st Corps	Gettysburg (1863)	Directing troops in battle
Major General John Sedgwick	6th Corps	Spotsylvania (1864)	Enemy sharpshooter
Major General Isaac Stevens	Division	Chantilly (1862)	Leading a charge
Major General Philip Kearny	Division	Chantilly (1862)	Accidentally rode behind enemy line
Major General Jesse Reno	Division	South Mountain (1862)	Leading an advance
Major General Israel Richardson	Division	Antietam (1862)	Artillery shell during battle
Major General Amiel Whipple	Division	Chancellorsville (1863)	Enemy sharpshooter
Major General Hiram Berry	Division	Chancellorsville (1863)	Directing troops in battle
Brevet Major General James Wadsworth	Division	Wilderness (1864)	Leading men in battle
Brevet Major General David Russell	Division	3rd Winchester (1864)	Artillery shell while leading men in battle
Brigadier General William Wallace	Division	Shiloh (1862)	While directing a retreat
Brigadier General Thomas Williams	Division	Baton Rouge (1862)	Directing troops in battle
Brigadier General James Jackson	Division	Perryville (1862)	Directing troops in battle
Brigadier General Isaac Rodman	Division	Antietam (1862)	Directing troops in battle
Brigadier General Thomas Stevenson	Division	Spotsylvania (1864)	Enemy sharpshooter
Brevet Brigadier General James Mulligan	Division	2nd Winchester (1863)	Enemy sharpshooter

CONFEDERATE

Name	Command	Battle	Manner of Death
General Albert Sidney Johnston	Department	Shiloh (1862)	Directing troops in battle
Lieutenant General Leonidas Polk	Corps	Pine Mountain (1864)	Artillery shell

Lieutenant General Thomas Jackson	Corp	Chancellorsville (1863)	Returning to line after reconnaissance
Lieutenant General Ambrose Hill	Corp	Petersburg (1865)	Between enemy lines
Major General J. E. B. Stuart	Corp	Yellow Tavern (1864)	Directing troops in battle
Major General Patrick Cleburne	Division	Franklin (1864)	Directing troops in battle
Major General Robert Rhodes	Division	3rd Winchester (1864)	Directing troops in battle
Major General William HT Walker	Division	Atlanta (1864)	Between enemy lines
Major General William Pender	Division	Gettysburg (1863)	Artillery shell
Major General James Gordon	Brigade	Meadow Bridge (1864)	Directing troops in battle
Major General John Pegram	Division	Hatcher's Run (1865)	Directing troops in battle
Major General Stephen Ramseur	Division	Cedar Creek (1864)	Directing troops in battle

THE ECONOMICS OF WAR—MONEY AND LIFE

"The war was expensive to the South as well as to the North, both in blood and treasure, but it was worth all it cost."

—Union General Ulysses S. Grant in his memoirs[144]

As in all wars, there were the monetary as well as human costs. It was estimated that the war's price tag for the North was about $6.2 billion, compared to about $4 billion for the South. These numbers significantly increased, even doubled, by 1940 due to pension payments to all Federal veterans and their widows in the years following the war. State governments and private contributions paid pensions for Confederate veterans and their widows until legislation was passed in 1958 that provided for Federal pension payments to two surviving Southern veterans and to the widows of 526 Confederate soldiers.

Prior to the start of the war, Northern states owned well more than 70 percent of the total wealth of the United States. Most of this inequity was because the North had more than five times the manufacturing capacity of the South, where the economy was primarily based on agriculture and dependent on the institution of slavery. Although 40 percent of the population of Southern states was slaves, only about 25 percent of white families owned slaves. When the Union blockaded the majority of Southern ports, the European market for cotton all but dried up, which led to growing financial hardship in the Confederacy throughout the war.

In addition to using money from the United States Treasury, the Union was able to successfully finance the war by enacting a series of fiscal measures, including the institution of an income tax, increases in other taxes and import tariffs, and issuance of bonds. The North also issued paper money called greenbacks, or legal tender, which were backed by government credit rather than gold, government reserves, or deposits.

The Confederacy did not fare so well in its ability to successfully finance the war. Since states' rights was a fundamental tenet of secession, the Confederate government never enacted an income tax, leaving it up to each state to determine income tax rates and the amount of money it would contribute to the central government, which was never enough to cover the growing war debt. Without a market to sell their goods, Southern farmers lost most of their income and were unable to pay taxes.

The Confederacy and Southern state governments alike printed their own currency, which undermined the economy by causing meteoric inflation. By the war's end, it took from sixty to seventy Confederate dollars to equal a gold dollar. In contrast, at the height of inflation in the North, it took only $2.59 to purchase a gold dollar. "To-day for a pair of forlorn shoes, I have paid $85," the Southern diarist Mary Chestnut wrote in her diary on February 1, 1864. "Mr. Petigru says you take your money to the market in the market basket, and bring home what you buy in your pocket-book."[145]

TEST YOUR KNOWLEDGE ABOUT
THE COST OF THE WAR

1. Virginia suffered the most major battles and engagements during the Civil War. Which state had the second most?

   a. Georgia   b. Missouri
   c. Kentucky   d. Tennessee
   e. Alabama

2. Who said, "There is many a boy here who looks on war as all glory, but, boys, it is all hell"?

   a. Ulysses S. Grant   b. Robert E. Lee
   c. William T. Sherman   d. Philip Sheridan
   e. Abraham Lincoln

3. By the end of the war, how much had it cost the Northern economy?

   a. $4.2 billion   b. $6.2 billion
   c. $8.2 billion   d. $10.2 billion
   e. $12.2 billion

4. Who was the highest-ranking commanding general on either side to be killed in battle?

   a. Thomas "Stonewall" Jackson
   b. James McPherson
   c. John Reynolds
   d. Leonidas Polk
   e. Albert Sidney Johnston

5. What percentage of the Southern population (not including Border States) in the 1860 census were slaves?

a. 20%   b. 30%

c. 40%   d. 50%

e. 60%

6. How many Union soldiers were killed in battle or from wounds received in battle?

a. 110,070   b. 150,238

c. 201,001   d. 100,731

e. 125,572

7. How many Confederate soldiers were killed in battle or from wounds received in battle?

a. 50,820   b. 62,777

c. 74,524   d. 80,333

e. 132,704

8. About how many total engagements (battles, skirmishes, etc.) were fought during the war?

a. 14,500   b. 12,500

c. 10,500   d. 8,500

e. 6,500

9. Which Confederate regiment suffered the highest percentage of loss in a single battle?

a. 1st Texas   b. 3rd North Carolina

c. 23rd North Carolina   d. 26th North Carolina

e. 6th Mississippi

10. During which battle did the regiment identified in #9 above suffer the highest percentage of loss in a single battle?

a. Antietam   b. Gettysburg

c. Shiloh   d. Chickamauga

e. Fredericksburg

CHAPTER SEVEN

Civil War Prisons

> *"It is hard on our men held in Southern prisons not to exchange them, but it is humanity to those left in the ranks to fight our battles. Every man we hold, when released on parole or otherwise, becomes an active soldier against us at once either directly or indirectly. If we commence a system of exchange which liberates all prisoners taken, we will have to fight on until the whole South is exterminated."*

> —Communication from Lieutenant General Ulysses S. Grant
> to Major General Benjamin Butler, August 18, 1864[146]

For much of the war, the two sides struggled to establish a uniform method to parole or exchange prisoners of war. Exchange meant that designated prisoners would be traded on each side. Parole meant that a prisoner would remain free but refrain from fighting until informed that they had been exchanged for a prisoner or parolee on the other side. In July 1862, a formal agreement was made between both sides that was specific enough to designate the value of each rank infantry and naval rank in the service, as shown in Figure 7.1.

Three factors all but stopped prisoner exchanges during the last half of the war. The first was Confederate President Jefferson Davis's declaration on December 24, 1862, that black troops and

FIGURE 7.1: EXCHANGE VALUE OF INFANTRY AND NAVAL RANKS [147]	
Commanding General or Admiral	60 privates or common seamen
Major General or Flag Officer	40 privates or common seamen
Brigadier General or Commodore	20 privates or common seamen
Colonel or Navy Captain	15 privates or common seamen
Lieutenant Colonel or Naval Commander	10 privates or common seamen
Major or Lieutenant Commander	8 privates or common seamen
Army Captain or Naval Lieutenant or Master	6 privates or common seamen
Lieutenant or Master's Mate	4 privates or common seamen
Naval Midshipmen or Warrant Officers, Merchant Vessel Master, or Commander of Privateer	3 privates or common seamen
Army Noncommissioned Officers, Naval Petty Officers, or Merchant Vessel Second Captains, Lieutenants or Mates	2 privates or common seamen

their commanding officers would not be treated as prisoners of war but would be turned over to state governments to be tried for servile insurrection. The second was when the Confederate Congress ordered the trial and execution of any captured white Union officer who led black troops. The third was Ulysses Grant's order in spring 1864 to suspend prisoner exchange in order to cut the flow of able troops to the remaining Confederate armies to support his strategy

FIGURE 7.2: CIVIL WAR PRISONS [148]					
UNION					
Site	Open	Built for	Max Held	# Died	Location
Alton	Feb '62	800	1,891	1,534	Alton, IL
Camp Chase	Jul '61	4,000	9,400	2,260	Columbus, OH
Camp Douglas	Feb '62	6,000	12,000	4,454	Chicago, IL
Camp Morton	Feb '62	2,000	5,000	1,763	Indianapolis, IN
Elmira	Jun '64	5,000	9,400	2,963	Elmira, NY
Fort Delaware	Jul '61	2,000	12,500	2,460	Pea Patch Island, DE
Fort McHenry	1861	600	*	33	Baltimore, MD
Johnson's Island	Feb '62	1,000	3,200	235	Sandusky Bay, OH
Nashville	1863	*	*	359	Nashville, TN
Old Capitol	Aug '61	1,500	2,763	457	Washington, DC
Point Lookout	Aug '63	10,000	22,000	3,584	Point Lookout, MD
Rock Island	Dec '63	10,000	8,594	1,960	Rock Island, IL
CONFEDERATE					
Andersonville	Feb '64	10,000	32,899	12,919	Andersonville, GA
Belle Isle	Jun '62	3,000	10,000	300+	Richmond, VA
Blackshear	Nov '64	5,000	5,000	*	Blackshear, GA
Cahaba	1863	500	3,000	225	Cahaba, AL
Camp Ford	Aug '63	*	4,900	286	Tyler, TX
Castle Pinckney	1861	150	300	*	Charleston, SC
Castle Thunder	1862	1,400	3,000	*	Richmond, VA
Danville	1863	3,700	4,000	1,300	Danville, VA
Florence	Sep '64	*	1,500	2,973	Florence, SC
Libby	Jul '61	1,000	4,221	*	Richmond, VA
Salisbury	Dec '61	2,500	10,000	3,963	Salisbury, NC
* = information not available					

of war by attrition. All three of these factors increased the suffering of prisoners during the last two years of the war.

Figure 7.2 shows a list of Union and Confederate prisoner-of-war camps and significant information concerning them.

CAMP SUMTER—ANDERSONVILLE, GEORGIA

"Over a hundred fifty dying per day now, and twenty-six thousand in camp. Guards shoot now very often. Boys, as guards, are the most cruel. It is said that if they kill a Yankee they are given a thirty days furlough."

—Union Prisoner First Sergeant John Ransom, July 8, 1864[149]

Confederate authorities put slaves to work in January 1864 clearing land for a new prison, Camp Sumter, outside of Anderson Station, Georgia. They used trees they cut down for a fifteen-foot-high stockade. Plans initially called for building barracks inside the sixteen-and-a-half-acre stockade, but, by 1864, the government could not afford to purchase and transport the lumber to this remote location. Instead, the enclosure was left open. A five-foot-wide creek running through the guards' camp before entering the stockade was the primary source of water for all the prisoners. As prisoners began to arrive, the water quickly became polluted with human waste and other contaminants from the guards' camp, leading to many deaths from dysentery and diarrhea.

The first prisoners arrived on February 25, 1864. They scrounged scraps of wood found within the stockade to build crude huts. Prisoners who arrived later used blankets and anything else they could find to construct lean-tos as a means to provide some form of protection from the elements.

It took only a matter of months to fill the prison to the point where the stockade had to be enlarged to include an additional ten acres, raising the estimated capacity to ten thousand men. Within weeks of completing the extension, almost thirty thousand men were confined within the prison.

The camp was now more than 1,600 feet long and 780 feet wide. Sentry stations were built at intervals of every 30 feet and a "deadline," a crude fence, extended all along the interior about 19 feet from the wall. Crossing the deadline meant almost certain death for any prisoner. Union prisoner John McElroy wrote that:

> "The first man was killed the morning after the Dead-Line was put up... Hardship and exposure had crazed him and brought on a severe attack of St. Vitus's dance [jerky, uncontrollable movements]. As he went hobbling around with a vacuous grin upon his face, he spied an old piece of cloth lying on the ground inside the Dead Line. He stooped down and reached under for it. At that instant the guard fired. The charge of ball-and-buck entered the poor old fellow's shoulder and tore through his body. He fell dead, still clutching the dirty rag that had cost him his life."[150]

Andersonville Prison (litho) by English School (20th century) (Private Collection/Ken Welsh/The Bridgeman Art Library)

Although rations were inadequate from the first days of the camp, they regularly diminished the longer the men were there due to shortages throughout the South and the lack of money to purchase necessary amounts to feed the prisoners. Their initial ration of sweet potatoes and meat eventually ended, and the amount of cornmeal they received was far less than required to sustain life. In addition to diarrhea and dysentery, many prisoners eventually succumbed to scurvy.

Once Atlanta fell to Union troops, Andersonville, about 120 miles to the south, was threatened. Transfer of prisoners to other camps began in September 1864, leaving fewer than 1,400 men—those too weak or sick to move—in the prison by December 1864. In fewer than 10 months, 13,000 men died as a result of being imprisoned at Andersonville. Figure 7.3 shows a partial list of the reported cases of sickness and death at the prison.

FIGURE 7.3: SICKNESS AND DEATH AT ANDERSONVILLE FROM MARCH 1 TO AUGUST 31, 1864 [151]		
Disease	# of Cases	# of Deaths
Fever (Malaria/Typhoid)	3,955	398
Diarrhea and Dysentery	16,772	4,529
Tuberculosis	114	33
Rheumatism	866	20
Scurvy	9,501	999
Bronchitis	2,808	90
Pneumonia and Pleurisy	979	266
Other Diseases and Injuries	7,691	1,377
Total	42,686	7,712

CAMP DOUGLAS—CHICAGO, ILLINOIS

"As if to add insult to injury, an observatory was erected just outside the gate of our prison, and spectators were permitted, for a sum of ten cents, to ascend to an elevated platform, where, with the aid of spy or field glasses furnished by the proprietors,

they could look down upon, and inspect us as objects of curiosity, as they would wild beasts in a menagerie."

—Confederate Prisoner Griffin Frost[152]

Not quite as infamous as Andersonville, Camp Douglas gained the reputation of being the worst of a number of poorly run prisoner-of-war camps in the North. Originally built outside of Chicago to temporarily house new recruits, prisoners began to arrive on February 21, 1862 (soldiers who surrendered following the capture of Forts Henry and Donelson, Tennessee). By the end of the month, more than 4,300 captives had arrived.

Camp Douglas was a series of compounds spread out over 60 acres and enclosed by a 6-foot-high fence. The compound holding the prisoners covered about 20 acres, upon which 64 crude wooden barracks were constructed.

A lack of proper drainage in the prison compound created large pools of swampy, standing water—breeding grounds for many diseases. The conditions were such that the U.S. Sanitary Commission called for the closing of the camp if a proper drainage system was not installed. Efforts finally were taken to improve the sanitary conditions of the camp in June 1863, but these changes never completely solved the problem.

By spring 1863, the mortality rate of the camp rose to more than 10 percent a month, which was higher than any other prisoner-of-war camp either North or South, including Andersonville. Figure 7.4 shows a list of the diseases and their effects on the inmates of Camp Douglas.

Unlike the commanders of Confederate prison camps, the availability of food, especially in the later stages of the war, was not a problem at Camp Douglas or any other prison in the North, but its distribution often was used as a means to control behavior. Reports of the horrendous conditions Union prisoners faced in Southern camps also affected the amount of food given to prisoners at Camp Douglas.

FIGURE 7.4: EFFECTS OF DISEASE IN CAMP DOUGLAS [153]		
Disease	# of Cases	# of Deaths
Fevers (Malaria/Typhoid)	15,938	1,407
Diarrhea and Dysentery	13,455	698
Anemia	585	4
Tuberculosis	259	113
Rheumatism	3,212	37
Scurvy	3,745	39
Bronchitis	1,628	27
Pneumonia and Pleurisy	4,655	1,296
Other Diseases and Injuries	26,611	388
Total	70,088	4,009

Since the camp was not originally constructed to house a prison, the level of security was below standard for a prison camp. The number of attempted escapes, therefore, increased as the conditions in the camp worsened due to overcrowding, harsh weather, and disease. By the time the camp closed in 1865, more than three hundred inmates had escaped.

Following the surrender of the Confederate armies, the remaining inmates willing to take an oath of allegiance to the United States were released and provided with transportation home. Those unwilling to take the oath—more than 1,700 Confederates—were released but had to find their own way home. By July 5, 1865, the last day for the remaining guards, only sixteen inmates were left in the hospital, too sick to travel. The camp was officially closed and demolished by the end of November 1865.

LIBBY PRISON—RICHMOND, VIRGINIA

"The water we are compelled to drink is from the James river, which on account of the recent rains, is warm and muddy. Add to all this the filth and nauseating stench of these apartments, which decency forbids us to describe. All our rooms are overcrowded, so that in sections the sleepers are like sardines in a box. They are consequently compelled to lie spoon-fashion.

Occasionally throughout the night, as poor fellows feel shoulder and hip bones ache, we hear them cry, 'Spoon over to the right,' or 'Spoon over to the left,' when a turn-over of a whole broadside of sleepers has to be effected."

—Union Prisoner Louis Beaudry, Chaplain
5th New York Volunteer Cavalry[154]

More than five hundred Union prisoners of war marched through the streets of Richmond in March 1862 to a warehouse on the block between Cary and Dock streets along the James River. It was called Libby Prison for the last proprietor of the building, Luther Libby, who was suspected of being a Union sympathizer.

The 45,000-square-foot structure was actually a series of three buildings connected by inner doors and designated East, Middle, and West buildings. Each had three stories in the front and four in the back. Prisoners were kept on the upper two floors in six poorly furnished rooms with inadequate ventilation. Each room measured about 105 feet by 45 feet and held about a hundred inmates.

The Confederate Libby Prison for Prisoners of War at Richmond, Virginia, by Alexander Gardner (1821–82). (Private Collection/Peter Newark Military Pictures/The Bridgeman Art Library)

A hospital, kitchen, and guards' quarters occupied the first floor, and the basement contained dungeon-like rooms for prisoners who displayed disciplinary problems.

Officers and enlisted men were kept together in Libby until large numbers of prisoners started to arrive following the Peninsula Campaign in spring 1862. Officers remained at Libby, and enlisted men were transferred to Belle Isle in the James River within sight of Libby Prison. By the end of 1862, conditions worsened as the prison population began to surpass the thousand-man capacity. As food became scarce across the Confederacy, the prisoners suffered from hunger and disease.

Published in the *New York Herald* in November 28, 1863, was a statement titled "The Richmond Prisoners," from four surgeons recently released from Libby. The article inflamed readers across the North and helped to reassess the Union's handling of Confederate prisoners, increasing their hardships in Northern prisons.

"We, the undersigned, surgeons of the United States Army, and recently prisoners in Richmond, Va., consider it our duty to publish a few facts that came to our knowledge while we were inmates of the hospital attached to Libby Prison .... As a result of our observations, we hereby declare our belief that since the battle of Chickamauga the number of deaths per diem has averaged fully fifty. The prevailing diseases are diarrhea, dysentery and typhoid pneumonia. Of late the percentage of deaths has greatly increased, the result of causes that have been long at work—as insufficient food, clothing and shelter, combined with that depression of spirits brought on so often by long confinement...

Thus we have over ten per cent of the whole number of prisoners held classed as sick men, who need the most assiduous and skillful attention; yet, in the essential matter of rations, they are receiving nothing but corn bread and sweet potatoes. Meat is no longer furnished to any class of our prisoners except to the few officers in Libby hospital, and all sick or well officers or privates are now furnished with a very poor article of corn bread in place of wheat bread, unsuitable diet for hospital patients prostrated with diarrhea, dysentery and fever, to say nothing of the balance of startling instances of individual suffering and horrid pictures of death from protracted sickness and semi-starvation we have had thrust upon our observation...

We leave it for others to say what is demanded by this state of things. The rebel daily papers in general terms acknowledged the truth of all we have affirmed, but usually close their abusive editorials by declaring that even such treatment is better than the invading Yankees deserve. The Examiner, in a recent article, begrudged even the little food the prisoners did receive and the boxes sent to us from home, and closed by eulogizing the system of semi-starvation and exposure as well calculated to dispose of us. All this is true; and yet cold weather has hardly commenced. We are horrified when we picture the wholesale misery and death that will come with the biting frosts of winter."[155]

Attempts to escape from Libby increased as conditions worsened, and a number of prisoners succeeded. The most successful attempt was led by Colonel Thomas Rose on February 9, 1864. Accompanied by 108 companions, Rose escaped through a 53-foot-long tunnel below the prison. Fifty-nine members of this group eventually made it to freedom. Forty-eight, including Rose, were recaptured, and two drowned.

Most of the prisoners in Libby were transferred south before the city fell to Union troops in April 1865. Former Confederate soldiers and officials were housed in the prison until August 3, 1868. The building was purchased in 1888 by a group of Chicago businessmen and moved to that city, where it was rebuilt. It housed the Libby Prison War Museum until 1895, when it was torn down and sections were sold as souvenirs.

JOHNSON'S ISLAND—SANDUSKY, OHIO

"The cold snap, as it is called here, exceeds anything of the kind I ever experienced in my life. I was afraid to walk from one end of the enclosure to the other for fear my blood would congeal and I would freeze to death. Water froze in our canteens under our heads and we suffered much for this element of life from the fact that the pumps were frozen, and the water supply which was at all times inadequate was cut short."

—Confederate Prisoner Colonel R. F. Webb,
6th Regiment North Carolina[156]

In February 1862, Confederate prisoners began to arrive at Johnson's Island, the prison camp constructed on an island in Sandusky Bay about three miles west of Sandusky, Ohio, following the capture of Forts Henry and Donelson. Barracks enclosed by a sixteen-and-a-half-acre stockade were intended to hold officers only, but both officers and enlisted men were held there until July 1862 when it became an officers-only camp until the end of the war. Built to hold about a thousand prisoners, the maximum population was about 3,200 men.

Prisoners lived in twelve barracks. When the barracks were unable to hold all the Confederate officers sent there, tents were pitched in the prison yard.

Lack of adequate water drainage was a serious problem the prisoners had to contend with. The soil was made of a mixture of clay and loam, which extended two to eight feet deep before resting on a base of limestone rock. A military inspector stated in a March 2, 1865, report:

"Owing to the geological formation sinks cannot be dug more than eight feet deep, and blasting to a greater depth is extremely difficult, owing to the character of the rock and the position of its strata. It follows that in a few weeks' time the

sinks become full and new pits have to be opened. This has been so often repeated that the ground north and south of the prison barracks for a distance of fifty feet on either side may now be considered as one continuous sink, very superficially covered, and saturating the whole ground down to the rock. At my inspection these sinks were in the filthiest condition imaginable, the excrementitious matter in some of them rising high above the seat and covering the floor."[157]

One of the harshest winters to hit that area of the country occurred in 1863–64. Poorly constructed barracks and a shortage of blankets and fuel caused a great deal of suffering among the prisoners. However, despite shortages and long, cold winters, the death rate at Johnson's Island was one of the lowest at any Union or Confederate prison. Fewer than three hundred prisoners died on the island during the course of the war. Figure 7.5 shows the numbers of cases of disease and death on the island during a period of twenty-five months.

FIGURE 7.5: SICKNESS AND DEATH AT JOHNSON'S ISLAND [158]		
Disease	# of Cases	# of Deaths
Fevers (Malaria/Typhoid)	670	53
Diarrhea and Dysentery	1,855	46
Anemia	35	1
Tuberculosis	14	7
Rheumatism	106	1
Scurvy	58	0
Bronchitis	57	1
Pneumonia and Pleurisy	99	25
Other Diseases and Injuries	803	27
Total	3,697	161

TEST YOUR KNOWLEDGE ABOUT
CIVIL WAR PRISONS

1. Which prisoner-of-war camp was infamous for having the highest mortality rate of any Union or Confederate camp?

   a. Elmira, New York
   b. Andersonville, Georgia
   c. Point Lookout, Maryland
   d. Camp Douglas, Illinois
   e. Libby Prison, Virginia

2. How many privates were necessary to be exchanged for the release of a major general?

   a. 10   b. 20
   c. 30   d. 40
   e. 50

3. How many privates were necessary to be exchanged for the release of an infantry captain?

   a. 2   b. 4
   c. 6   d. 8
   e. 10

4. When did Andersonville Prison open?

   a. February 1861   b. February 1862
   c. February 1863   d. February 1864
   e. February 1865

5. For how many months was Andersonville an active prisoner-of-war camp?

a. 50   b. 40

c. 30   d. 20

e. 10

6. Identify whether the following prisoner-of-war camps held Union or Confederate prisoners.

 a. Camp Douglas   b. Andersonville

 c. Libby Prison   d. Johnson's Island

 e. Belle Isle

7. What was the source of the most deaths at Andersonville?

 a. Scurvy   b. Pneumonia

 c. Rifle fire   d. Fevers

 e. Dysentery

8. What was the source of the most deaths at Camp Douglas?

 a. Scurvy   b. Pneumonia

 c. Rifle fire   d. Fevers

 e. Dysentery

9. Libby Prison was actually a series of how many buildings connected by inner doors?

 a. 2   b. 3

 c. 4   d. 5

 e. 6

10. Johnson's Island is located three miles away from which Ohio city?

 a. Cleveland   b. Erie

 c. Sandusky   d. Toledo

 e. Columbus

CHAPTER EIGHT

Ten Interesting Characters and Events of the Civil War

SAM DAVIS—BOY HERO OF THE CONFEDERACY

"If I had a thousand lives, I would give them all before I would betray my friends or the confidence of my informer."

—Response by Sam Davis when asked to save his life by revealing the source of the documents he carried when captured[159]

On the morning of November 27, 1863, twenty-one-year-old Sam Davis, convicted of being a Confederate spy, sat on a coffin in the back of the wagon carrying him through the streets of Pulaski, Tennessee, to the gallows on East Hill, where he was to be hanged. Arriving at its destination, the wagon stopped, and Davis, his legs shackled, was helped out. He sat under a tree, awaiting the signal to mount the steps to the scaffold.

While waiting, Davis asked the Union Provost Marshal, Captain W. F. Armstrong, for any word from the front. He was told about the Confederate defeat at Missionary Ridge outside of Chattanooga, Tennessee, two days earlier, to which Davis expressed regret and stated, "The boys will have to fight the rest of the battles without me."[160] Not long after, he was told it was time.

When war broke out, Davis had enlisted in the 1st Tennessee Volunteer Infantry and fought in Virginia before his regiment returned to Tennessee and took part in the Battle of Shiloh in April 1862. The battles of Perryville, Kentucky, in August 1862 and Stones River, Tennessee, in December 1862 followed.

Not long after Stones River, Davis transferred to the Coleman's Scouts, a Confederate intelligence force led by a family friend, Captain Henry Shaw, General Braxton Bragg's Chief of Scouts. The group got its name from the fact that Shaw used "E. C. Coleman" as a pseudonym on all his dispatches.

Davis was captured on November 20, 1863, carrying a dispatch, concealed in his shoe, from Shaw to Bragg giving the dispositions of Union troops at Nashville. Refusing to answer the questions of Provost Marshal Armstrong, he was taken to Brigadier General Grenville

Dodge. The general immediately realized that some of the dispatches had been stolen from his own desk and demanded to know the identity of E. C. Coleman. Davis refused to provide the information.

The next day, November 21, Davis again was brought to Dodge's office. The general told him that he realized that Davis was just a messenger and that if he revealed Coleman's identity, he would set Davis free. Unknown to the Union authorities, they already held Shaw in their jail in Pulaski. When Davis again refused to identify Shaw as Coleman, Dodge advised Davis that he would be court-martialed and most likely sentenced to die if he did not cooperate. Davis responded:

"I know that I will have to die, but I will not tell where I got the information, and there is no power on earth that can make me tell. You are doing your duty as a soldier, and I am doing mine. If I have to die, I do so feeling that I am doing my duty to God and my country."[161]

He was court-martialed and sentenced to death. The day before his hanging, Davis wrote the following:

"Dear Mother: Oh, how painful it is to write you! I have got to die to-morrow morning—to be hanged by the Federals. Mother, do not grieve for me. I must bid you good-by forevermore. Mother, I do not fear to die. Give my love to all.

Your son, Samuel Davis"[162]

When Davis reached the top of the gallows steps, Armstrong said, "I regret very much having to do this; I feel that I would almost rather die myself than to do what I have to do." Davis answered, "I do not think hard of you; you are doing your duty."[163] He was asked one more time to reveal Coleman's identity, but refused.

Davis is buried behind his family home, which has been turned into a museum for him in Smyrna, Tennessee. A bronze statue of Davis was dedicated in 1909 on the grounds of the Tennessee State Capitol in Nashville.

HENRY AND CLARA RATHBONE—
THE LAST GUESTS OF THE LINCOLNS

"I long ago made up my mind that if anybody wants to kill me, he will do it. If I wore a shirt of mail, and kept myself surrounded by a body-guard, it would be all the same. There are a thousand ways of getting at a man if it is desired that he should be killed."

—Statement made by President Lincoln to journalist
Noah Brooks in the summer of 1863[164]

Abraham and Mary Lincoln had invited Lieutenant General Ulysses S. Grant and his wife, Julia, to Ford's Theater on April 14, 1865, to see the British comedy *Our American Cousin*. The Grants declined under the pretense that they would be traveling, but it actually was because Mrs. Grant felt belittled in the past by Mrs. Lincoln. Many believed that Mrs. Lincoln was jealous of the attention given to Grant following the surrender of Robert E. Lee five days earlier.

Several other couples were invited but also declined. Finally, twenty-seven-year-old Major Henry Rathbone and his nineteen-year-old fiancée, Clara Harris, accepted. Rathbone entered the war in 1861 and rose to the rank of major of the 12th United States Regular Infantry Regiment by war's end. After his father's death, his mother married Judge Ira Harris, who was appointed senator from New York when William Seward became Lincoln's secretary of state. Clara was Ira Harris's daughter and, therefore, had become Rathbone's stepsister before their engagement.

Rathbone and his fiancée rode in a carriage together with the Lincolns to Ford's Theater. They arrived late. The play was suspended, and "Hail to the Chief" played as the Presidential party made its way—to much applause—to the flag-draped box to the right of the stage. Lincoln bowed to the audience before sitting in an armchair next to his wife. Clara sat at the far end of the box, with Rathbone to her left.

When he heard a shot and saw the President slump forward in his chair, Rathbone jumped up and struggled with Lincoln's assassin. John Wilkes Booth pulled out a hunting knife, cut Rathbone in the head, and made a long, deep gash in the major's arm. Rathbone's efforts threw Booth off balance and helped cause the assassin to break his leg when he hit the stage after jumping from the box.

Afterward, Clara comforted Mrs. Lincoln while they took shelter in the front parlor of a house across the street from Ford's Theater while the President lay dying in a rear bedroom. Rathbone had collapsed from his wounds and was taken for treatment.

Rathbone remained in the army for two more years before resigning and marrying Clara on July 11, 1867. The couple had three children. The family moved to Germany when Rathbone was named U.S. Consul to Hanover in 1882. His mental health, affected by the wounds he received during Lincoln's assassination and pangs of guilt for not having saved the President's life, had deteriorated over the years, leading Rathbone to struggle with severe depression and psychotic behavior. He had hoped that the move to Germany would improve his state of mind, but it did not. Little more than a year after the move, on December 23, 1883, he shot his wife to death and threatened the lives of their children before attempting suicide by stabbing himself. After he was taken into custody, his children were sent back to the United States to live with a maternal uncle.

Rathbone was tried and convicted in German courts of murder, but also was found to be insane and committed to an asylum for the criminally insane in Hildesheim, Germany, where he remained until his death on August 14, 1911. He was buried in the Hanover city cemetery next to his wife's grave. In 1952, after years of neglect and lack of any family contact, the cemetery association ordered that Rathbone's and Clara's bodies be disinterred and their bones destroyed to make more room in the cemetery.

SERGEANT RICHARD KIRKLAND— ANGEL OF MERCY

"The sergeant stopped at the door and said: 'General, can I show a white handkerchief?' The general slowly shook his head, saying emphatically, 'No, Kirkland, you can't do that.' 'All right,' he said, 'I'll take the chances,' and ran down with a bright smile on his handsome countenance."

—Confederate Brigadier General Joseph Kershaw's last exchange with Sergeant Richard Kirkland before the sergeant crossed over the stone wall to administer to wounded Union soldiers at Marye's Heights after the Battle of Fredericksburg[165]

Many men exhibited acts of heroism before the stone wall at the base of Marye's Heights just west of Fredericksburg, Virginia, on December 13, 1862. After all, seven divisions attacked the Rebel position starting at about noon and ending after 5:00 p.m. When the attacks ended, almost eight thousand Union soldiers were killed, wounded, or captured. The night after the attack, the battlefield was a no-man's-land with Confederate and Yankee soldiers looking for any opportunity to kill another enemy while Union wounded lay where they fell exposed to the winter cold without aid. No one on either side was willing to risk his life tending to the suffering who issued agonizing cries of "Water! Water!" until the next afternoon.

Early in the afternoon of December 14, Confederate Brigadier General Joseph Kershaw, who commanded this portion of the line along the stone wall, was approached by Sergeant Kirkland of the 2nd South Carolina:

> "General! I can't stand this .... All night and all day I have heard those poor people crying for water, and I can stand it no longer. I come to ask permission to go and give them water."[166]

The general reminded Kirkland of the danger of climbing the wall, but the nineteen-year-old soldier would not be deterred. Kershaw finally gave in and granted the soldier's wish. The youth left anxiously, but soon hesitated and returned, asking if he could wave a white handkerchief as he crossed over the stonewall. Unwilling to risk confusion in his front with a sign commonly associated with surrender, Kershaw said no. Unfazed, Kirkland gathered and filled as many canteens as he could carry and set off on his humanitarian mission.

Kershaw recounted this encounter with Kirkland in the January 29, 1880, edition of the Camden, South Carolina, newspaper *The News and Courier*. Reverend J. William Jones included Kershaw's letter in his 1887 book *Christ in Camp*. Although many witnessed the heroic actions of Kirkland that day, the story was not universally circulated among the public until Kershaw's letter was published. The retired general described the young sergeant's activity on the open field:

> "With profound anxiety he was watched as he stepped over the wall on his errand of mercy—Christ-like mercy. Unharmed he reached the nearest sufferer. He knelt beside him, tenderly raised the drooping head, rested it gently upon his own noble breast, and poured the precious life-giving fluid down the fever-scorched throat. This done, he laid him tenderly down, placed his knapsack under his head, straightened out his broken limb, spread his overcoat over him, replaced his empty canteen with a full one, and turned to another sufferer. By this

time his purpose was well understood on both sides, and all danger was over. From all parts of the field arose fresh cries of 'water, water; for God's sake, water!' More piteous still the mute appeal of some who could only feebly lift a hand to say there, too, was life and suffering.

For an hour and a half did this ministering angel pursue his labor of mercy, nor ceased to go and return until he relieved all the wounded on that part of the field. He returned to his post wholly unhurt. Who shall say how sweet his rest that winter's night beneath the cold stars!"[167]

Kirkland survived, untouched, the battles of Chancellorsville in May 1863 and Gettysburg in July 1863, after which he was promoted to the rank of lieutenant. His luck would finally run out, however, at the Battle of Chickamauga on September 20, 1863. He and a companion were in the lead during the attack on the Union position on Snodgrass Hill when he was mortally wounded.

He is buried in Quaker Cemetery in Camden, South Carolina, not far from Kershaw's grave. A magnificent statue of Kirkland administering to the wounded in front of the stone wall at Fredericksburg, sculpted by Felix deWeldon, the architect of the Iwo Jima memorial in Washington, D.C., was dedicated in 1965.

The meaning of Kirkland's heroic act at Fredericksburg was described perfectly by Kershaw at the end of his letter to the Camden newspaper:

"He was but a youth when called away, and had never formed those ties from which might have resulted a posterity to enjoy his fame and bless his country; but he has bequeathed to the American youth—yea, to the world—an example which dignifies our common humanity."[168]

AMBROSE BIERCE—THE MYSTERIOUS
DEATH OF THE SOLDIER AND JOURNALIST

*"After firing his shot, Private Carter Druse reloaded his rifle
and resumed his watch. Ten minutes had hardly passed when
a Federal sergeant crept cautiously to him on hands and knees.
Druse neither turned his head nor looked at him, but lay
without motion or sign of recognition.*

'Did you fire?' the sergeant whispered.

'Yes.'

'At what?'

*'A horse. It was standing on yonder rock—pretty far out. You
see it is no longer there. It went over the cliff.'*

*The man's face was white, but he showed no other sign of
emotion. Having answered, he turned away his eyes and said
no more. The sergeant did not understand.*

*'See here, Druse,' he said, after a moment's silence, 'it's no use
making a mystery. I order you to report. Was there anybody on
the horse?'*

'Yes.'

'Well?'

'My father.'

*The sergeant rose to his feet and walked away. 'Good God!'
he said."*

—The end of Ambrose Bierce's story *A Horseman in the Sky*
about a Union soldier, while on guard duty, killing
his father, a Confederate officer[169]

Eighteen-year-old Ambrose Gwinnett Bierce enlisted in the 9th
Indiana Volunteer Infantry on April 19, 1861, four days after the
first call for volunteers. Thus began the military career of one of
the few successful writers to serve a full term of service during the

war. His postwar works captured the horrors of battle better than any other contemporary author.

Bierce's fearlessness on the battlefield was evident during his first action at Grafton, West Virginia, in July 1861. A correspondent for the *Indianapolis Journal* wrote that Bierce and a comrade named Boothroyd charged up a hill:

> *"within fifteen paces of the enemy's breastworks when Boothroyd was wounded in the neck by a rifle ball paralyzing him. Bierce, in open view of the enemy, carried poor Boothroyd and his gun without other assistance fully twenty rods, balls falling around him like hail."*[170]

Bierce was an excellent observer of the oftentimes absurd circumstances of warfare. During the Battle of Shiloh in April 1862, Bierce, then a sergeant major, saw a woman on a steamboat that was carrying his regiment across the Tennessee into the heart of the battle:

> *"She was a fine creature, this woman; somebody's wife. Her mission, as she understood it, was to inspire the failing heart with courage; and when she selected mine I felt less flattered by her preference than astonished by her penetration. How did she learn? She stood on the upper deck with the red blaze of battle bathing her beautiful face, the twinkle of a thousand rifles mirrored in her eyes; and displaying a small ivory-handled pistol, she told me in a sentence punctuated by the thunder of great guns that if it came to the worst she would do her duty like a man! I am proud to remember that I took off my hat to this little fool."*[171]

While walking through the human and materiel carnage after the battle, Bierce's detachment came upon a wounded soldier. His description of the scene shows his later cynicism toward war and the way it shapes men's minds and actions:

"A Federal sergeant, variously hurt, who had been a fine giant in his time. He lay face upward, taking in his breath in convulsive, rattling snorts, and blowing it out in sputters of froth which crawled creamily down his cheeks, piling itself alongside his neck and ears. A bullet had clipped a groove in his skull, above the temple; from this the brain protruded in bosses, dropping off in flakes and strings. I had not previously known one could get on, even in this unsatisfactory fashion, with so little brain. One of my men, whom I knew for a womanish fellow, asked if he should put his bayonet through him. Inexpressibly shocked by the cold-blooded proposal, I told him I thought not; it was unusual, and too many were looking."[172]

Shortly after Shiloh, Bierce was commissioned a second lieutenant. In February 1863, he was promoted to first lieutenant and appointed acting topographical officer for Brigadier General William Hazen. Bierce went on to participate in many of the major battles in Tennessee and Georgia. He survived the disastrous charge of Hazen's brigade on May 27, 1864, against a heavily defended Confederate position at Pickett's Mill, Georgia. Half of Hazen's brigade were killed, wounded, or captured. He recounted this human slaughter in his biting story *The Crime at Pickett's Mill.*

Bierce was severely wounded less than a month later, during the Battle of Kennesaw Mountain, Georgia. While leading the skirmish line forward, a bullet hit him in the temple and passed along the side of his skull. The bullet was removed in surgery, but, as a result of the wound, he suffered pain and fainting spells for most of his remaining adult life.

He returned to service in time to participate in the battles of Franklin and Nashville in Tennessee, in November and December 1864, where he saw thousands of Confederates slaughtered as a result of appalling leadership. Those actions ended his participation in the war. He went on to great fame as a journalist and a popular writer of essays, satirical books, and twenty-five Civil War and numerous other horror short stories.

In October 1913, at the age of seventy-three, Bierce toured the old battlefields where he fought during the war. At the end of his tour, he decided to visit Mexico and follow Pancho Villa's revolutionary army. He disappeared during this visit, and his fate has never been discovered.

As cynical as he grew to the cold effects of war on its participants and the politicians who dictated its course, Bierce always considered his participation in the conflict as the high point of his life. In an article he wrote for the *San Francisco Examiner* in 1890, he stated:

> *"It was once my fortune to command a company of soldiers— real soldiers. Not professional life-long fighters, the product of European militarism—just plain, ordinary, American, volunteer soldiers, who loved their country and fought for it with never a thought of grabbing it for themselves; that is a trick which the survivors were taught later by gentlemen desiring their votes."*[173]

JOHNNY CLEM— THE DRUMMER BOY OF SHILOH?

"The story of Chickamauga would not be complete without the mention of Johnny Clem, the drummer-boy."

> —Mrs. Emma C. Cheney on Johnny Clem, a celebrity during and after the war and a popular subject in postwar books[174]

Walt Disney's Wonderful World of Color aired part one of the movie *Johnny Shiloh* on January 20, 1963, in the middle of the centennial anniversary of the Civil War. The movie told the story of a boy of about ten years old who ran away from home to join a volunteer regiment. He first attempted to join the 3rd Ohio Volunteer Infantry, but was rejected as too young. He then tried the 22nd Michigan, which had been traveling with the 3rd Ohio, but they also rejected him as too young. Undeterred, he stayed with the men from the 22nd Michigan and was taken in as a mascot. He was a drummer boy during the Battle of Shiloh, when his drum was smashed by a shell that knocked him unconscious. His friends found him, however, and gave him the name "Johnny Shiloh." Part two of the movie *Johnny Shiloh* aired the next Sunday, showing his courage during the Battle of Chickamauga.

Though the movie was earnest and impactful, the history it revealed was distorted and misleading—making for a sorry lesson for many who viewed the movie with awe and wonder. Though the movie was interesting, the real story of Johnny Shiloh is much more compelling—even though it leaves many questions unanswered.

John Joseph Klem was born on August 13, 1851. He would later change his name to John Lincoln Clem. When war broke out, he was only nine years old, but yearned to fight. Claims that he attempted to run away with the 3rd Ohio seem to be untrue, however, since the regiment only briefly passed through his home in Newark, Ohio, on its way to camp in June 1861. The first documented evidence of Johnny's involvement was the record of his being mustered into the 22nd Michigan on May 1, 1863, at the age of eleven well after the Battle of Shiloh.

Toward the end of the fighting on the second day of the Battle of Chickamauga on September 20, 1863, the 22nd Michigan, 21st Ohio, and 89th Ohio were left to hold off the advancing Rebel line along Snodgrass Hill while the other Union troops, who were not routed earlier in the day, withdrew from the field. With their ammunition spent, many of the soldiers in these three regiments were captured. In that group was Johnny Clem, but it was only later that a reported incident on the battlefield would make him one of the most recognized soldiers of the war.

Just like the mistaken credit for his performance during the Battle of Shiloh, the truth of what Clem really did on the field at Chickamauga is difficult to determine. A contemporary account of the incident was written by Benjamin Taylor for the Chicago *Journal* and reprinted in the Belmont *Chronicle*:

> "Late in the waning day, the waif left almost alone in the whirl of the battle, a rebel Colonel dashed up and looked down at him, ordered him to surrender: 'Surrender!' he shouted, 'you little d—n son of a —!' The words were hardly out of the rebel's mouth, when Johnny brought his piece to 'order arms,' and as his hand slipped down to the hammer, he crossed it back, swung up the gun to the position of 'charge bayonet,' and as the officer raised his saber to strike the piece aside, the glancing barrel lifted into range, and the proud Colonel tumbled dead from his horse, his lips fresh stained with the syllable of vile reproach he had flung upon a mother's grave in the hearing of her child."[175]

This scene was portrayed in the Disney movie, but a search of records shows that no Confederate colonel had been killed or wounded on the part of the field defended by the 22nd Michigan. There was an orderly, a Confederate private, who was wounded at the time and place consistent with Clem's story. No witnesses to the event ever came forward. Unlike many of his regiment, Clem was able to escape from the Confederates that night, and he made his way back to Chattanooga.

Clem received two minor wounds before autumn 1864, when he was discharged. He enrolled in high school and graduated in 1870. Clem was nominated to enter West Point by then-President Ulysses S. Grant, but repeatedly failed the entrance exam due to his lack of formal education. He moved to Washington, D.C., and was appointed a second lieutenant in the 24th United States Infantry with Grant's help. Clem served until his retirement as a colonel in the quartermaster corps in 1916, the last remaining Civil War veteran in active military service. Due to his longevity in the army and the celebrity of his Civil War service, a special act of Congress promoted him to the rank of major general after his retirement. He died in San Antonio, Texas, on May 13, 1937, and is buried at Arlington Cemetery with the words "Drummer Boy of Chickamauga" on his headstone.

ANGELO CRAPSEY—
A TRAGIC END TO A HEROIC LIFE

"When he first came back I remember that he did not appear as he had before his capture, appeared sort of strange and as if he wanted to be by himself. If I went to speak to him sometimes he would make answer and then again he would not say anything. I know that he used to say that he was unfit to be seen in decent company. [He] complained that his clothes and himself were lousy and called our attention to the matter when we knew that he [only] imagined what he was talking about. Once in a while he would get a spell when he would talk about how the prisoners had to suffer and about the vermin that they had to encounter while he was a prisoner. I know that he always acted strange after his return."

—Angelo Crapsey's friend Charlie Robbins recalling Crapsey's
behavior after returning from Libby Prison[176]

When returning from warfare, soldiers often seem very different to family and friends. Many labels have been used over the years to describe this postbattle malady: nostalgia, melancholia, soldier's heart, combat fatigue, and shell shock to name a few. Since the end of the Vietnam War, more attention has been given to this condition, and even another label has been attached to it: post-traumatic stress disorder. Its cause has been defined as a life-threatening event or one that severely affects the physical or emotional wellbeing of an individual. PTSD causes behavioral problems that can include an exaggerated startle response, forgetfulness, sleep disorders, violent outbursts, low self-esteem, and lack of confidence. Escape from basic life situations seems the goal of those suffering from PTSD, which often leads to severe psychotic disorder or even suicide. It is a subject now discussed openly, and any social stigma related to it is breaking down as people become more informed of its cause and effect. That was not the case in earlier wars, however, particularly during and after the Civil War.

Many Civil War veterans returned with a mental ailment that their family and friends could not understand, and it often resulted in institutionalization. "Nostalgia," or "soldier's heart," as it was often called, was not an uncommon experience for veterans returning from the Civil War. Angelo Crapsey's story shows how, in little more than three years, exposure to the rigors of army life, an enemy prison, and the horrors of battle transformed him from an eager and sheltered boy of nineteen years old to a man devastated by war and ready to end his life.

Like most young men looking for adventure, Crapsey was enthusiastic when he left home for the war and enlisted in the 13th Pennsylvania Reserves Infantry. His first letters were full of descriptions of army life, patriotism, and contempt for those who showed less than total commitment to winning the war. In one letter, he described the suicide of a Sergeant William Rehrig. Crapsey described him as being "shattered" by typhoid fever and detailed how Rehrig put the muzzle of his rifle in his mouth and pulled the trigger with his toe. In his letter, Crapsey expressed contempt for turning to suicide to escape the pain. As time passed, however, Crapsey's letters became darker with self-doubt and confusion, which ultimately would lead to his own attempts at escape.

Crapsey's regiment chased Confederate Major General Thomas "Stonewall" Jackson through the Shenandoah Valley in 1862 before joining Union Major General George McClellan in the Seven Days Campaign on the outskirts of Richmond, Virginia. He was exposed to much death and suffering in the spring and summer of 1862, but it was just a prelude to what he would experience in the next two battles: Antietam in September 1862, the bloodiest battle of the war, and Fredericksburg in December 1862. Crapsey was captured at Fredericksburg and sent to Libby Prison in Richmond. His stay at the prison was brief—only three weeks—but it had a lasting effect on him, as evidenced by Charles Robbins's description of Crapsey's return to the regiment featured at the beginning of this story.

Crapsey returned to his unit long enough to fight in the Battle of Gettysburg in July 1863, but was soon hospitalized with fever and dysentery. The illness was serious enough that Crapsey was released from the army. His participation in the Civil War was over, but his internal conflict was intensifying. Once he returned home, his family found little resemblance to the young man who left for war little more than two years before. Violent outbursts and frequent attempts at suicide, drinking poison and attempted drowning, convinced them that he needed institutionalization. Before that could be arranged, however, he was successful in his final attempt to take his life on August 4, 1864. Patterning his actions on those of Sergeant Rehrig, Crapsey stuck the muzzle of a rifle in his mouth and fired it with his toes. His fight with the mental anguish that had been torturing him had ended.

The wonder is that not all soldiers return home shattered by what they experience in war, but that so many go on to lead successful lives. Of course, many do not, however. There are unknown numbers of Angelo Crapseys after warfare. Some take their own lives, while others have just enough strength to live their remaining days in constant mental anguish. A study by the National Institutes of Aging on the Civil War service records of 15,072 men revealed that 43 percent of the veterans had mental health problems following the war.

JAMES ANDREWS AND WILLIAM FULLER—
THE GREAT LOCOMOTIVE CHASE

*"The people of the State [Georgia] have been informed through
the medium of the public press of the facts connected with the
daring attempt made by a band of spies, sent by the authority
of the enemy, to burn the bridges on the W. & A. Railroad.
The conduct of Mr. Fuller, the conductor, and of some others in
the hazardous pursuit, while the spies were in possession of
the train, deserves the highest commendation, and entitles
them to the consideration of the General Assembly. I therefore
recommend the appointment of a committee of the two houses
to enquire into the facts and report upon them, and that such
medals or other public acknowledgment be awarded to the
parties whose conduct was most meritorious, as will do justice
to their services, and stimulate others to like deeds of daring
when necessary for the public security."*

—October 1862 speech by Georgia Governor
Joseph Brown recognizing William Fuller's
tenacity in the pursuit of *The General*[177]

On May 7, 1961, *Walt Disney's Wonderful World of Color* showed the
first part of a black-and-white movie, *Andrews Raiders: Secret
Mission*. This was followed the next week by *Andrews Raiders:
Escape to Nowhere*. The Civil War centennial celebration had just
begun, and scores of children were glued to the television on
Sunday nights to see what new stories Walt Disney would tell.
Many were taken with the tale of the Great Locomotive Chase, and,
in particular, the heroism of the raid's leader, James Andrews.

Walt Disney produced only a handful of Civil War movies
during the 1960s. Another was *Johnny Shiloh*, shown in two parts
in January 1963, discussed earlier in this chapter. Unlike *Johnny
Shiloh* and other "factual" stories shown on *Wonderful World of
Color*, *Andrews Raiders* remained mostly true to the actual story.

That may be because it was first produced as a theatrical movie in 1956 called *The Great Locomotive Chase*.

The actual event occurred on April 12, 1862. Union Major General Ormsby Mitchel realized that it would be impossible to capture the strategic rail center of Chattanooga, Tennessee, without blocking the Confederates' ability to send reinforcements by rail from Atlanta. Civilian scout James Andrews proposed a daring plot to travel deep into Georgia, commandeer a train, and, while traveling north between Atlanta and Chattanooga, destroy tracks and bridges along the way. He recruited another civilian, William Campbell, and twenty-two Union soldiers to accomplish the plan.

The group traveled south in pairs, in civilian clothes, and met in Marietta, Georgia, to execute their plan. All but two men made it to Marietta. The two who did not enlisted in a Confederate artillery battery to avoid being identified as spies. The remaining raiders boarded a passenger train, heading north, pulled by the

The Great Locomotive Chase. (Private Collection/Peter Newark Military Pictures/The Bridgeman Art Library)

locomotive *The General*, in Marietta on April 12. Andrews and his men seized the engine and several boxcars while the train's crew stopped at Big Shanty, Georgia. *The General*'s conductor, William Fuller, discovered the train pulling out of the station while he was eating breakfast and set off in pursuit on foot.

Andrews's advance north in *The General* was slowed as his men tore tracks and cut telegraph lines. They also were forced to remain on *The General*'s regular timetable in order to avoid suspicion in the cities along the way. In the meantime, Fuller and two companions remained in hot pursuit, commandeering handcars and three locomotive engines along the way. Pursuit looked hopeless, but Fuller pressed on. Just past Ringgold, Georgia, about ninety miles from their starting point, the raiders, unable to stop to secure more fuel because of Fuller's close pursuit, were forced to abandon the train.

In less than two weeks, all of the raiders were captured. Andrews, Campbell, and six of the Union soldiers were tried and hanged in Atlanta. Andrews suffered a particularly painful death since the drop from the scaffold to the ground was not much greater than his six-foot height, causing a slow death by strangulation instead of a broken neck.

Eight of the raiders escaped, and the others were exchanged. All but two of the Union participants received the first Congressional Medals of Honor for their participation in the raid. Andrews and Campbell were ineligible for the medal because of their civilian status.

Not only were Andrews's raiders immortalized in the Walt Disney film, but also in three other films before that: the 1911 one-reeler *The Railroad Raiders of '62*; the 1915 movie *The Railroad Raiders of '62*, which used scenes from the 1911 film; and the 1927 Buster Keaton movie *The General*. In the latter, which has little relevance to the actual event, Keaton portrays Johnnie Gray, who chases the hijacked train because the love of his life, Annabelle Lee, is aboard. Although Andrews is a character in *The General*, there is no mention of Fuller.

The General's conductor received some recognition during and after the war in parts of the South, but his daring exploit never approached the fame achieved by James Andrews. It isn't the story of just one man, however. The combined devotion of these two heroes to their cause is what makes the tale of the great locomotive chase endure.

CONFEDERATE GENERAL CLEMENT EVANS— THE SEWING KIT THAT SAVED HIS LIFE

"The wounds from the Minié balls can readily be distinguished, by the long conical shape of the cut. The Minié ball generally strikes to kill."

—Medical report of effect of being struck by Minié ball[178]

Being wounded on the battlefield was often a greater fear than death for a Civil War soldier. It didn't take a surgeon to realize that anyone struck in the head or torso most likely would die. Those soldiers often were left untreated in field hospitals while surgeons worked instead on the wounded who had a chance to live.

If a bullet crushed an arm or leg bone, amputation was often the only option. In most cases, flesh wounds were not mortal, but infection caused by surgeons examining the wounds with dirty, bloody bare hands could lead to gangrene and death. It was not until well after the Civil War that doctors came to understand the problems caused by unsanitary conditions in an operating room.

Bullets striking objects kept in uniform pockets, such as coins, bibles, and diaries, often saved lives. The same was true when bullets struck items hanging from the shoulder or belt, such as bayonets, buckles, and cap boxes. It was not often, however, that sewing kits saved lives. Fortunately, such was the case for Confederate Brigadier General Clement Evans at the Battle of Monocacy, Maryland, on July 9, 1864.

Evans was a prodigy. Born on February 25, 1833, he was a lawyer at age eighteen and a judge at twenty-two. He enlisted in the 31st Georgia Infantry and became its colonel in April 1862. He suffered through typhoid, dysentery, and several other ailments during the war. Prior to the Battle of Monocacy, he had been wounded four times, though not seriously.

When the Confederate left flank was threatened during the Battle of Monocacy, Evans's brigade was called in to attack the enemy along that section of the line. Bitter fighting occurred in a wheatfield of the Thomas Farm, with Evans losing many men killed and wounded. He was struck twice during the fight. One bullet passed through his left arm without hitting a bone. The other struck him in the chest. A sewing kit Evans had been carrying in his pocket slowed the bullet enough that it lodged in his side. The impact of the hit sent several pins deep into his body. His men carried him off the field in a blanket to the Confederate lines across the Monocacy. Surgeons removed the bullet from his side, but many of the pins were so deep that it took years for them to self-extract.

Had it not been for the fact that Evans chose to carry a sewing kit into battle, his life most likely would have ended at Monocacy. Although he was not fully recovered, he returned to service about three months later and was present when Confederate General Robert E. Lee surrendered the Army of Northern Virginia at Appomattox Court House, Virginia, in April 1865.

ALONZO CUSHING—A 147-YEAR WAIT FOR THE CONGRESSIONAL MEDAL OF HONOR

"Cushing ran down the last of his guns to the battle-line.
The rest had been smashed to scrap by Lee's artillery fire.
He held his guts in his hand as the charge came up the wall
And his gun spoke out for him once before he fell to the ground."

—Stephen Vincent Benet's *John Brown's Body*[179]

At about 1:00 p.m. on July 3, 1863, the third day of the Battle of Gettysburg, Pennsylvania, one hundred and fifty pieces of Confederate artillery opened on the middle of the Union line along Cemetery Ridge. Directly in the center of the target were the six cannon of twenty-two-year-old Lieutenant Alonzo Cushing's Battery A, 4th United States Artillery. His guns, as well as most of the others along the Union position, opened fire on the Rebel artillery. By the cannonade's end, more than two hours later, four of Cushing's guns were disabled and all his officers were dead or wounded. He also suffered two grievous wounds during the shelling, one to his right shoulder and the other, in what appeared to be a mortal wound, to his abdomen and groin.

Ordered to retire his battery and seek medical aid, Cushing refused to leave the field. He sought and received permission to move his guns forward to an angle in a fence, which would become appropriately named the "Bloody Angle." He continued to direct his guns as twelve to fourteen thousand Confederates advanced toward his position. He struggled to hold his lacerated bowels in his hand while guiding his gunners.

He stood on a fence with his field glasses directing fire, held up by his battery sergeant, Frederick Fuger. As Cushing gave the order to fire canister, a bullet entered his mouth and exited through the back of his skull, killing him instantly. Left with all officers dead or disabled, Fuger took command of the battery and directed that his gunners fire double and triple rounds of canister into the enemy line. This was accomplished by putting more than one charge of canister in the cannon at a time. When the Confederates overran his guns, Fuger ordered his remaining men to fight hand to hand until reinforcements assisted in turning the Rebels back.

After the battle, Fuger was appointed second lieutenant of the battery and remained with the unit through the rest of the war and into the postwar, retiring as a major of the 4th Artillery in June 1900. More than thirty-four years after the battle, on August 24,

1897, he was awarded the Congressional Medal of Honor for his actions at Gettysburg.

Cushing's family and friends and members of the 71st Pennsylvania Volunteers who fought with the 4th US Artillery at Gettysburg erected a small monument to him in 1887, on the field where he fought his last battle. It states:

Erected in honor of
Lt. A. H. Cushing
And his 4th U.S. Battery A.
by
Col. R. Penn Smith
and his Regiment
71st PA. Vol's.

The reader may ask why Cushing wasn't awarded the Congressional Medal of Honor for his actions on that day. It was very rare for someone to receive the medal posthumously in the early years of the medal. Figure 8.1 details the awarding of the medal over the years.

The policy for awarding the medal posthumously has changed over the years; it has been more the norm than the exception since World War II.

In 2002, a movement began to recognize the contribution Cushing made at Gettysburg. Senator Russ Feingold of Wisconsin nominated Cushing for the Medal of Honor, and the U.S. Army recommended the medal in May 2010. An Act of Congress is necessary to award the medal to the young artillery lieutenant 147 years after his tremendous heroism in battle. It was expected to be passed in late 2010 or early 2011, in time for the beginning of the Civil War Sesquicentennial. Whether he is finally awarded the medal, however, his deeds and sacrifice live on at the Bloody Angle in Gettysburg.

FIGURE 8.1: MEDAL OF HONOR WINNERS

War	Totals	Posthumous	% Received Posthumously
Civil War (1861–65)	1,522	32	2.1%
Indian Campaigns (1867–91)	426	13	3.1%
Korea (1871)	15	0	0.0%
Spanish American (1898)	110	1	0.9%
Samoa (1898–99)	4	0	0.0%
Philippine Insurrection (1899–1902)	80	4	5.0%
Philippine Outlaws (1911)	6	0	0.0%
Boxer Rebellion (1900)	59	1	1.7%
Mexican Campaign (1914–17)	56	0	0.0%
Haiti (1914)	6	0	0.0%
Dominican Republic (1914)	3	0	0.0%
World War I (1917–18)	124	33	26.6%
Haiti (1919–20)	2	0	0.0%
Nicaraguan Campaign (1928–32)	2	0	0.0%
World War II (1941–45)	464	266	57.3%
Korean War (1950–53)	133	95	71.4%
Vietnam (1959–75)	246	154	62.6%
Somalia (1993)	2	2	100.0%
Afghanistan (2001–)	3	3	100.0%
Iraq (2003–)	4	4	100.0%
Noncombat	193	5	2.6%
Unknowns	9	9	100.0%
GRAND TOTALS	3,469	622	17.9%

THE LAST REUNION OF THE BLUE AND THE GRAY—AND THE YEARS BEYOND

"In great deeds something abides. On great fields something stays. Forms change and pass; bodies disappear, but spirits linger, to consecrate ground for the vision-place of souls. And reverent men and women from afar, and generations that know us not and that we know not of, heart-drawn to see where and by whom great things were suffered and done for them, shall

come to this deathless field to ponder and dream; And lo! the
shadow of a mighty presence shall wrap them in its bosom, and
the power of the vision pass into their souls. This is the great
reward of service. To live, far out and on, in the lives of others."

—Joshua Chamberlain, speaking at the dedication of the
Monument to the 20th Maine, October 3, 1889,
Gettysburg, Pennsylvania[180]

From June 29 to July 4, 1938, 1,359 Union and 486 Confederate veterans met in Gettysburg, Pennsylvania, in what was to become the last major reunion of Civil War veterans. Those dates included the seventy-fifth anniversary of the Battle of Gettysburg, fought July 1 to July 3, 1863. The average age of these men was ninety-four years old. Although all of the veterans attending had to show proof of belonging to a Union or Confederate unit during the war, only sixteen of them, eleven Yankees and five Rebels, actually were present at Gettysburg during the battle.

Veteran representatives came from all states except Rhode Island, with three attending from Canada. All were housed in a tent city on the grounds of Gettysburg College and were treated to a variety of activities during the six days, including a five-mile-long parade through the streets of Gettysburg; the recreation of Pickett's Charge with one Confederate veteran of the battle and a handful of Union veterans shaking hands on the spot where their comrades fought hand to hand seventy-five years earlier; the dedication of the Eternal Light Peace Memorial by President Franklin D. Roosevelt; and a demonstration of America's military might on the eve of World War II.

An even larger reunion had taken place at Gettysburg twenty-five years earlier from June 29 to July 6, 1913. A total of 53,407 veterans attended and were treated to a parade, a recreation of Pickett's Charge, and a display of America's military might on the eve of World War I. President Woodrow Wilson attended, but the most popular visitor proved to be Major General Daniel Sickles, one of the central characters of the battle and the man given the most credit for creating the Gettysburg National Military Park while a member of Congress. It would turn out to be a last hurrah for the controversial general, who died on May 3, 1914.

Figure 8.2 illustrates statistics from the two reunions:

FIGURE 8.2: STATISTICS FROM GETTYSBURG REUNIONS		
Category	1913	1938
Union Attendees	44,713	1,359
Confederate Attendees	8,694	486
Authorized Attendants for Veterans	0	1,845
Veteran Deaths During Reunion	9	1
Tents	6,592	2,679
Kitchens	173	3
Street Lights	500	396
Drinking Fountains	32	40
Cots	44,850	8,425
Wool Blankets	102,262	19,400
Pies	7,000	1,223
Pounds of Cream of Wheat & Wheatena	21,153	1,200
Pounds of Butter	12,383	3,796
Dozens of Eggs	24,930	11,060
Pounds Fresh Beef	156,410	15,865
Pounds of Fowl	14,722	12,090
Pounds of Coffee	12,206	200
Pounds of Macaroni	3,500	120
Gallons of Ice Cream	2,015	3,203

Civil War veterans came to Gettysburg in 1913 and 1938 for any number of reasons. Some were returning and others were coming for the first time. In 1913, national unity was an important theme for the reunion. In 1938, the last hurrah was the greatest draw for these ninety-plus-year-old veterans. For all, however, at both reunions, the opportunity to traipse over ground that they and their fellow soldiers made sacred was a special opportunity they could not pass up.

During the 1913 reunion, Dr. Nathaniel Cox, Chairman of Indiana's Gettysburg Reunion Commission, stated the following in a speech during a commemorative service for all veterans:

> *"Comrades and friends, these splendid statues of marble and granite and bronze shall finally crumble to dust, and in the ages to come, will perhaps be forgotten, but the spirit that has called this great assembly of our people together, on this field, shall live forever."*[181]

On a visit to the battlefield of Gettysburg in 1909, a West Point cadet, George S. Patton, who later went on to become one of the heroes of the Allied victory in World War II, wrote:

> *"The trenches are still easily seen and their grass grown flower strewn slopes agree ill with the bloody purpose for which they were designed and used. Nature covers up the scars of earth far better than those of men. There is to me strange fascination in looking at the scenes of the awful struggles which raged over this country. A fascination and a regret. I would like to have been there too."*[182]

Those marble, granite, and brass testaments to the fight that took place across the fields of Gettysburg have not yet crumbled to dust, parts of the terrain remain scarred by the fight, and the memories of the reunions of the veterans of this and all the other battles of the Civil War have not faded. Luckily, as Joshua Chamberlain stated in his 1889 address, whether you are a veteran, military cadet, or a young boy or girl:

> *"In great deeds something abides. On great fields something stays. Forms change and pass; bodies disappear, but spirits linger, to consecrate ground for the vision-place of souls."*[183]

TEST YOUR KNOWLEDGE ABOUT THE CHARACTERS AND EVENTS OF THE CIVIL WAR

1. Which city is Sam Davis from?

   a. Pulaski, Tennessee
   b. Smyrna, Tennessee
   c. Knoxville, Tennessee
   d. Memphis, Tennessee
   e. Nashville, Tennessee

2. Who were the Lincolns' first choice to join them at Ford's Theater to see *Our American Cousin* on the night of April 14, 1865?

   a. Mr. and Mrs. William Seward
   b. Henry Rathbone and Clara Harris
   c. Mr. and Mrs. Robert E. Lee
   d. Mr. and Mrs. Ulysses S. Grant
   e. Mr. and Mrs. John Booth

3. In which battle did Sergeant Kirkland earn the name Angel of Mercy?

   a. Gettysburg
   b. Chickamauga
   c. Fredericksburg
   d. Antietam
   e. Vicksburg

4. In which battle did Ambrose Bierce receive the wound from which the effects plagued him most of his life?

   a. Chattanooga, Tennessee
   b. Shiloh, Tennessee
   c. Pickett's Mill, Georgia
   d. Franklin, Tennessee
   e. Kennesaw Mountain, Georgia

5. Which regiment adopted Johnny Clem?

   a. 3rd Ohio   b. 22nd Michigan
   c. 8th Ohio   d. 21st Ohio
   e. 23rd Michigan

6. To which Confederate prison was Angelo Crapsey taken after being captured during the Battle of Fredericksburg?

   a. Andersonville, Georgia
   b. Belle Isle, Virginia
   c. Libby Prison, Virginia
   d. Castle Thunder, Virginia
   e. Salisbury Prison, North Carolina

7. What was the name of the locomotive that James Andrews and his raiders commandeered on April 12, 1862?

   a. *The Texas*   b. *The Admiral*
   c. *The Carolina*   d. *The General*
   e. *The Jefferson Davis*

8. How many wounds did Confederate General Clement Evans receive during the war?

   a. 3   b. 4
   c. 5   d. 6
   e. 7

9. Which artillery unit did Union Lieutenant Alonzo Cushing command?

   a. Battery A, 2nd US Artillery
   b. Battery C, 4th US Artillery
   c. Battery A, 4th US Artillery
   d. Battery D, 4th US Artillery
   e. Battery B, 3rd US Artillery

10. In what year did Franklin Roosevelt dedicate the Eternal Light Peace Memorial?

a. 1913

b. 1930

c. 1936

d. 1938

e. 1940

Glossary

A or Wedge tent—Made of canvas, this tent sloped down from a ridge pole held up by poles at each end. About fifty square feet in size, it held four men.

Acoustic shadow—Atmospheric conditions that blocked the sound of a battle from an observer a short distance away while the echoes of artillery could be heard many miles further from the fighting.

Adjutant—Staff officer with the primary responsibility for transmitting orders.

Battle Above the Clouds—The attack of Union soldiers on Confederate positions on Lookout Mountain, Tennessee, on November 24, 1863. Clouds cloaked the summit of the mountain during the battle.

Bell tent—Another name for a Sibley tent.

Bohemian—Newspaper reporter or illustrator traveling with an army.

Bounty—Money paid by federal and/or state governments to induce men to enlist. The figure increased as military service lost its popularity as the war progressed.

Breach—Hole in battle line or fortification usually caused by enemy artillery or infantry attack.

Breech-loading rifle—Ammunition loaded at the breech, between the stock of the gun and the barrel.

Brevet—An honorary, temporary promotion in rank often due to meritorious service in combat. It did not entitle the recipient to receive the pay associated with the brevet rank.

Buck and ball—A .69 caliber cartridge used in smoothbore rifles made up of three buckshot and a one-ounce ball wrapped in paper above a charge of gunpowder.

Caisson—Two-wheeled gun carriage that could carry two chests of ammunitions and a spare wheel.

Canister—Tin cylinder ammunition for artillery, which carried cast iron balls or other shards of metal packed in four tiers of sawdust. Shells for howitzers could hold as many as forty-eight pieces of metal. Very effective for defending against close-range infantry attacks.

Cap—Small piece of paper or metal with gunpowder placed over the nipple of a gun, which is struck by the hammer to produce a spark to fire the gun.

Carbine—Shorter than a rifle, this firearm was a lightweight weapon used principally by cavalry.

Cartridge—Bullet and powder wrapped in a paper or metal container for use in muskets, rifles, and carbines.

Colors—National or unit flag used to orient soldiers in and out of battle.

Commissary—Staff position with the responsibility of ordering, storing, and issuing food to troops.

Desiccated vegetables—Brick of a variety of vegetables with all water removed. Used primarily in stews and soups.

Dog tent—Two pieces of canvas that, when attached together, formed a small A-frame tent. Two soldiers would carry one piece of the canvas.

Drawers—Underwear.

Embalmed beef—Canned beef ration.

Enfilade fire—Fire into the flank of an enemy line perpendicular to your own.

Foot cavalry—Reference to infantry, particularly Union and Confederate units, known for long, quick marches, such as the famous Rebel "Stonewall Brigade."

Friendly fire—Incidents when infantry, artillery, or cavalry mistakenly fire at their own units.

Gatling gun—Invented by Richard Gatling, this hand-cranked, .577-caliber weapon had six revolving rifle barrels and could fire as many as six hundred rounds per minute.

Guidon—Flag designating a company or troop of cavalry or light artillery.

Hardtack—A three-inch square, quarter-inch-thick biscuit. In storage, they became extremely hard and often were infested with insects. Soldiers often soaked them in water or coffee before trying to bite into them.

Haversack—Multipurpose white canvas, waterproofed, lined storage bag carried over the shoulder.

Housewife—Little sewing kits carried by soldiers to patch and repair uniforms and shoes.

Howitzer—A smoothbore artillery piece produced in sizes large enough to fire 12-, 24-, 32-, or even 50-pound shells.

Kepi—Forage caps of French design, which were round, made of various-sized crowns, and featured a leather visor. Common headwear for both Union and Confederate troops.

Knapsack—Made of black rubberized cloth or painted cotton cloth or canvas. A blanket roll, poncho, portion of shelter tent, oil cloth, and personal items were either strapped on it or stored inside. Fully packed, it would weigh between thirty and fifty pounds and was carried on the back.

Limber—Two-wheeled carriage that could carry a chest of artillery ammunition. Smaller than a caisson.

Medal of Honor—Authorized by Congress in December 1861, it was the only medal to recognize valor in battle. Congress awarded 2,384 of the medals for actions during the Civil War, but the qualifications were loosely applied, including awarding it to 864 men in the 27th Maine for remaining active for four days past their expiration of service. In 1917, Congress rescinded 911 metals, most from the Civil War, including all those awarded to men in the 27th Maine.

Meet the elephant—First experience in battle.

Minié ball—Soft lead bullet with cone shaped base for rifled muskets. Invented by Claude-Étienne Minié, this projectile exited the muzzle of a musket with a spin that multiplied its accuracy over use of the round balls of smoothbore muskets.

Noncombatants—Individuals who traveled with an army but did not fight, such as chaplains, surgeons, journalists, sutlers, etc.

Picket pin—Foot-long iron fastener carried by cavalrymen to be driven into the ground to tether their horses.

Quaker gun—Logs hewn and painted black to look like artillery pieces to deceive enemy troops.

Quartermaster—Staff officer whose primary responsibility was to provide clothing, equipment, lodging, and transportation, when necessary, for his unit.

Rammer—Wooden block on the end of a long wooden staff used to drive charge down the bore of an artillery piece. A sponge was on the other end of the staff, which, when wet, was used to extinguish any sparks in the bore before loading it again.

Ramrod—Metal or wooden staff stored under a musket or rifle and used to drive a charge down the bore of the gun.

Reveille—Morning drum or bugle call notifying troops to wake up.

Rifling—Grooves cut into the length of a musket, rifle, carbine, or artillery piece to stabilize the spin and flight of a fired projectile.

Salient—Fortified position that extends in front of a line of battle. Commanders would create salients in their lines to defend a position which, if occupied by the enemy, could endanger their own lines.

Salt beef and pork—Beef or pork preserved using dry salt or brine. This process draws deadly microorganisms out of the meat by removing most of the water present in the meat.

Sibley tent—Invented in 1857 by Major Henry Sibley, this was a large cone-shaped canvas tent with a center pole support and an opening at the top for ventilation in summer and a stove opening in the winter. Similar to an American Indian teepee and could accommodate as many as twenty men.

Spherical case shot—Thin-walled lead or iron shell filled with as many as seventy-eight smaller metal balls surrounding a charge of gun powder at the center. The shell was ignited by a timed fuse with a maximum burn time of five seconds. When ignited, the shell spewed metal shards in all directions.

Stand of Colors—The position of a single regimental flag in battle. Union regiments carried two flags into battle: the familiar American flag with thirteen red and white stripes and thirty-five stars on a blue background (the flag contained thirty-four stars until West Virginia was admitted to the Union in 1863) and a regimental flag with a blue background and an eagle in the center. Confederate regiments carried one flag into battle, the Stars and Bars, which took several different forms, the most familiar being a blue Saint Andrew's cross with thirteen stars on a red background carried by the Army of Northern Virginia.

Strategy—Plans developed by military commanders to cover the execution of a battle, campaign, and war.

Sutlers—Civilians who followed regiments during the war and offered those items for sale not typically provided by the government, such as food products, tobacco, newspapers, and cutlery. Strict rules covered their conduct in an attempt to protect soldiers from unscrupulous storekeepers.

Tactics—The deployment of troops in battle.

Thumb stall—Buckskin cushion filled with horsehair worn over the thumb to protect it while covering a cannon vent while being sponged or loaded.

Wall tent—Similar shape as the Wedge or A tent but halfway down the side, the side drops vertically to the ground, forming a wall. It had a long fly, or canvas overhang, extending in front of the entrance to the tent to shelter tables from the elements.

Zouave—Colorful type of Union and Confederate uniform adapted from the French army. Distinctive pieces of clothing included fezzes or turban hats, short jackets with elaborate trim and braid, vest, very baggy pants, and leggings.

Recommended Reading

Many subjects relating to the war have been covered in this book. It is hoped that the information provided has sparked the reader's interest in one or more of these topics. A list of books on the war is presented below and has been divided into categories to assist in identifying works that will provide greater insights into areas of interest. The versions listed should be readily available at bookshops or online.

THE LIFE AND EXPERIENCES OF THE COMMON UNION AND CONFEDERATE SOLDIER

Coco, Gregory A. *The Civil War Infantryman: In Camp, On the March, and in Battle*. Thomas Publications, 1996.

Galwey, Thomas Francis. *The Valiant Hours*. The Stackpole Company, 1961.

Wiley, Bell Irvin. *The Life of Billy Yank: The Common Soldier of the Union*. Louisiana State University Press, 2008.

Wiley, Bell Irvin. *The Life of Johnny Reb: The Common Soldier of the Confederacy*. Louisiana State University Press, 2007.

WEAPONS AND EQUIPMENT

Coates, Earl J. and Thomas, Dean S. *An Introduction to Civil War Small Arms*. Thomas Publications, 1996.

Hess, Earl J. *The Rifle Musket in Civil War Combat: Reality and Myth*. University Press of Kansas, 2008.

Thomas, Dean S. *Cannons: An Introduction to Civil War Artillery*. Thomas Publications, 1996.

CIVIL WAR BATTLES

Bearss, Edwin C. *Fields of Honor: Pivotal Battles of the Civil War*. National Geographic, 2007.

Civil War Preservation Trust. *Civil War Sites, 2nd: The Official Guide to the Civil War Discovery Trail*. Globe Pequot, 2007.

Kennedy, Frances H., Editor. *The Civil War Battlefield Guide*. The Conservation Fund, 1998.

BATTLE OF FIRST BULL RUN

Davis, William C. *Battle at Bull Run: A History of the First Major Campaign of the Civil War*. Louisiana State University Press, 1981.

Gottfried, Bradley M. *The Maps of First Bull Run: An Atlas of the First Bull Run (Manassas) Campaign*. Savas Beatie, 2009.

Riddleburger, Sam and Hemphill, Michael. *Stonewall Hinkleman and the Battle of Bull Run*. Dial, 2009.

MONITOR VS. *MERRIMACK*

Clancy, Paul. *Ironclad: The Epic Battle, Calamitous Loss, and Historic Recovery of the USS Monitor*. International Marine/Ragged Mountain Press, 2005.

Mulligan, Tim and Holzer, Harold. *The Battle of Hampton Roads: New Perspectives on the USS Monitor and the CSS Virginia*. Fordham University Press, 2006.

Nelson, James L. *Reign of Iron: The Story of the First Battling Ironclads, the Monitor and the Merrimack*. Harper Paperbacks, 2005.

BATTLE OF SHILOH

Cunningham, Edward, Joiner, Gary, and Smith, Timothy B. *Shiloh and the Western Campaign of 1862*. Savas Beatie, 2009.

Daniel, Larry J. *Shiloh: The Battle that Changed the Civil War*. Simon & Schuster, 1998.

McDonough, James Lee. *Shiloh—In Hell Before Night*. University of Tennessee Press, 1977.

SEVEN DAYS BATTLES

Dougherty, Kevin and Moore, J. Michael. *The Peninsula Campaign of 1862: A Military Analysis*. University Press of Mississippi, 2010.

Gallagher, Gary W. *The Richmond Campaign of 1862: The Peninsula and the Seven Days*. The University of North Carolina Press, 2008.

Sears, Stephen W. *To the Gates of Richmond: The Peninsula Campaign*. Mariner Books, 2001.

BATTLE OF SECOND BULL RUN

Hennessy, John J. *Return to Bull Run: The Campaign and Battle of Second Manassas*. University of Oklahoma Press, 1999.

Langellier, John and Adams, Mike. *Second Manassas 1862: Robert E. Lee's Greatest Victory*. Osprey Publishing, 2002.

Martin, David G. *The Second Bull Run Campaign: July–August 1862*. Da Capo Press, 2003.

BATTLE OF ANTIETAM

McPherson, James M. *Crossroads of Freedom: Antietam*. Oxford University Press, 2002.

Priest, John M. *Antietam: The Soldiers' Battle*. Oxford University Press, 1994.

Sears, Stephen W. *Landscape Turned Red: The Battle of Antietam*. Mariner Books, 2003.

BATTLE OF FREDERICKSBURG

Gallagher, Gary W. *The Fredericksburg Campaign: Decision on the Rappahannock*. The University of North Carolina Press, 2007.

O'Reilly, Francis A. *The Fredericksburg Campaign: Winter War on the Rappahannock*. Louisiana State University Press, 2006.

Rable, George C. *Fredericksburg! Fredericksburg!* The University of North Carolina Press, 2001.

THE BATTLE OF STONES RIVER

Cozzens, Peter. *No Better Place to Die: The Battle of Stones River*. University of Illinois Press, 1991.

McDonough, James L. *Stones River—Bloody Winter in Tennessee*. University of Tennessee Press, 1983.

Spruill, Matt and Spruill, Lee. *Winter Lightning: A Guide to the Battle of Stones River*. University of Tennessee Press, 2007.

BATTLE OF CHANCELLORSVILLE

Gallagher, Gary W. *Chancellorsville: The Battle and Its Aftermath*. The University of North Carolina Press, 2008.

Sears, Stephen W. *Chancellorsville*. Mariner Books, 1998.

Stackpole, Edward J. *Chancellorsville: Lee's Greatest Battle*. Stackpole Books, 1989.

THE BATTLE OF GETTYSBURG

Petruzzi, J. David. *The Complete Gettysburg Guide: Walking and Driving Tours of the Battlefield, Town, Cemeteries, Field Hospital Sites, and Other Topics of Historical Interest*. Savas Beatie, 2009.

Sears, Stephen W. *Gettysburg*. Mariner Books, 2003.

Trudeau, Noah A. *Gettysburg: A Testing of Courage*. Harper Perennial, 2003.

THE VICKSBURG CAMPAIGN

Ballard, Michael B. *Vicksburg: The Campaign That Opened the Mississippi*. The University of North Carolina Press, 2010.

Bearss, Edwin C. and Hills, J. *Receding Tide: Vicksburg and Gettysburg—The Campaigns that Changed the Civil War*. National Geographic, 2010.

Winschel, Terrence. *Triumph and Defeat: The Vicksburg Campaign*. Savas Beatie, 2004.

THE BATTLE OF FORT WAGNER

Emilio, Luis F. *The Assault on Fort Wagner, July 18, 1863: The Memorable Charge of the Fifty-fourth Regiment of Massachusetts Volunteers*. Kessinger Publishing, 2008.

Vierow, Wendy. *The Assault on Fort Wagner: Black Soldiers Make a Stand in South Carolina Battle*. PowerKids Press, 2004.

Wise, Stephen R. *Gate of Hell: Campaign for Charleston Harbor, 1863*. University of South Carolina Press, 1994.

THE BATTLE OF CHICKAMAUGA

Cozzens, Peter. *This Terrible Sound: The Battle of Chickamauga*. University of Illinois Press, 1996.

Powell, David. *The Maps of Chickamauga: An Atlas of the Chickamauga Campaign, Including the Tullahoma Operations, June 22–September 23, 1863*. Savas Beatie, 2009.

Woodworth, Steven E., Lundberg, John R., Mendoza, Alexander, and Powell, David. *The Chickamauga Campaign*. Southern Illinois University Press, 2010.

THE BATTLE OF CHATTANOOGA

Cozzens, Peter. *The Shipwreck of Their Hopes: The Battles for Chattanooga*. University of Illinois Press, 1996.

Woodworth, Steven E. *Six Armies in Tennessee: The Chickamauga and Chattanooga Campaigns*. Bison Books, 1999.

Woodworth, Steven E. *This Grand Spectacle: The Battle of Chattanooga*. State House Press, 1999.

THE BATTLE OF THE WILDERNESS

Rhea, Gordon C. *Cold Harbor: Grant and Lee, May 26–June 3, 1864.* Louisiana State University Press, 2002.

Rhea, Gordon C. *The Battles for Spotsylvania Court House and the Road to Yellow Tavern, May 7–12, 1864.* Louisiana State University Press, 2005.

Rhea, Gordon C. *The Battle of the Wilderness, May 5–6, 1864.* Louisiana State University Press, 2004.

THE ATLANTA CAMPAIGN

Castel, Albert E. *Decision in the West: The Atlanta Campaign of 1864.* University Press of Kansas City, 1995.

McMurry, Richard M. *Atlanta 1864: Last Chance for the Confederacy.* Bison Books, 2001.

Wortman, Marc. *The Bonfire: The Siege and Burning of Atlanta.* Public Affairs, 2009.

THE SIEGE OF PETERSBURG

Field, Ron. *Petersburg 1864–1865: The Longest Siege.* Osprey Publishing, 2009.

Hess, Earl J. *In the Trenches at Petersburg: Field Fortifications and Confederate Defeat.* The University of North Carolina Press, 2009.

Sommers, Richard J. *Richmond Redeemed: The Siege at Petersburg.* Doubleday, 1981.

THE SHENANDOAH VALLEY CAMPAIGN

Gallagher, Gary W. *The Shenandoah Valley Campaign of 1864.* The University of North Carolina Press, 2009.

Lepa, Jack H. *The Shenandoah Valley Campaign of 1864.* McFarland, 2010.

Wert, Jeffry. *From Winchester to Cedar Creek: The Shenandoah Campaign of 1864.* Southern Illinois University Press, 2010.

SHERMAN'S MARCH TO THE SEA

Davis, Burke. *Sherman's March: The First Full-Length Narrative of General William T. Sherman's Devastating March Through Georgia and the Carolinas.* Vintage, 1988.

Glatthaar, Joseph T. *The March to the Sea and Beyond: Sherman's Troops in the Savannah and Carolinas Campaigns.* Louisiana State University Press, 1995.

Trudeau, Noah A. *Southern Storm: Sherman's March to the Sea*. Harper Perennial, 2009.

HOOD'S TENNESSEE CAMPAIGN

Carpenter, Noel. *A Slight Demonstration: Decatur, October 1864, Clumsy Beginning of Gen. John B. Hood's Tennessee Campaign*. Legacy Books and Letters, 2007.

McDonough, James L. and Connelly, Thomas L. *Five Tragic Hours: Battle of Franklin*. University of Tennessee Press, 1984.

Sword, Wiley. *The Confederacy's Last Hurrah: Spring Hill, Franklin and Nashville*. University Press of Kansas, 1993.

CIVIL WAR PRISONS

Gillispie, James M. *Andersonvilles of the North: The Myths and Realities of Northern Treatment of Civil War Confederate Prisoners*. University of North Texas Press, 2008.

Kantor, MacKinlay. *Andersonville*. Plume, 1993.

Speer, Lonnie R. *Portals to Hell: Military Prisons of the Civil War*. University of Nebraska Press, 2005.

SURRENDER OF ROBERT E. LEE

Catton, Bruce. *A Stillness at Appomattox*. Anchor, 1990.

Chamberlain, Joshua. *The Passing of Armies: An Account of the Final Campaign of the Army of the Potomac*. Bantam, 1992.

Ellis, Edward S. *The Camp-Fires of General Lee, from the Peninsula to the Appomattox Court-House: With Reminiscences of the March, the Camp, the Bivouac and of Personal Adventure*. Nabu Press, 2010.

SURRENDER OF JOSEPH JOHNSTON

Bradley, Mark L. *The Battle of Bentonville: Last Stand In the Carolinas*. Da Capo Press, 1996.

Hughes, Nathaniel C. *Bentonville: The Final Battle of Sherman and Johnston*. The University of North Carolina Press, 1996.

Hughes, Nathaniel C. *This Astounding Close: The Road to Bennett Place*. The University of North Carolina Press, 2000.

CAPTURE OF JEFFERSON DAVIS

Cooper, William J. *Jefferson Davis, American*. Vintage, 2001.

Johnson, Clint. *Pursuit: The Chase, Capture, Persecution and Surprising Release of Jefferson Davis*. Citadel, 2009.

Swanson, James L. *Bloody Crimes: The Chase for Jefferson Davis and the Death Pageant for Lincoln's Corpse*. William Morrow, 2010.

RATHBONES AND LINCOLN'S ASSASSINATION

Good, Timothy S. *We Saw Lincoln Shot: One Hundred Eyewitness Accounts*. University Press of Mississippi, 1996.

Mallon, Thomas. *Henry and Clara: A Novel*. Picadore, 1995.

Steers, Edward, Jr. *Blood on the Moon: The Assassination of Abraham Lincoln*. The University Press of Kentucky, 2010.

AMBROSE BIERCE

Bierce, Ambrose. Thomsen, Brian M., Editor. *Shadows of Blue and Gray: The Civil War Writings of Ambrose Bierce*. Forge Books, 2003.

Morris, Roy, Jr. *Ambrose Bierce: Alone in Bad Company*. Oxford University Press, 1999.

O'Connor, Richard. *Ambrose Bierce: A Biography*. Little Brown and Company, 1967.

JOHNNY CLEM

Keesee, Dennis M. *Too Young to Die: Boy Soldiers of the Union Army 1861–1865*. Blue Acorn Press, 2001.

Wisler, G. Clifton. *When Johnny Went Marching: Young Americans Fight the Civil War*. Harper Collins, 2001.

CONFEDERATE GENERAL CLEMENT EVANS

Leepson, Marc. *Desperate Engagement: How a Little-Known Civil War Battle Saved Washington, D.C. and Changed American History*. St. Martin's Griffin, 2008.

Welsh, Jack D., M.D. *Medical Histories of Confederate Generals*. Kent State University Press, 1995.

Welsh, Jack D., M.D. *Medical Histories of Union Generals*. Kent State University Press, 1995.

PTSD AND THE CIVIL WAR VETERAN

Brandt, Dennis W. *Pathway to Hell: A Tragedy of the American Civil War*. University of Nebraska Press, 2008.

Dean, Eric T., Jr. *Shook over Hell: Post-Traumatic Stress, Vietnam, and the Civil War*. Harvard University Press, 1997.

Speer, Bill. *From Broomsticks to Battlefields*. Deeds Publishing, 2010.

THE GREAT LOCOMOTIVE CHASE

Bonds, Russell S. *Stealing the General: The Great Locomotive Chase and the First Medal of Honor.* Westholme Publishing, 2008.

Cohen, Stan. *The General and The Texas: A Pictorial History of the Andrews Raid, April 12, 1862.* Pictorial Histories Publications, 1999.

Rottman, Gordon. *The Great Locomotive Chase—The Andrews Raid 1862.* Osprey Press, 2009.

ALONZO CUSHING

Beyer, Walter. F. and Keydel, Oscar F., Editors. *Deeds of Valor: How America's Civil War Heroes Won the Congressional Medal of Honor.* Smithmark Publishers, 2000.

Cole, Philip M. *Civil War Artillery at Gettysburg.* Da Capo Press, 2002.

Newton, George W. *Silent Sentinels: A Reference Guide to the Artillery of Gettysburg.* Savas Beatie, 2005.

CIVIL WAR VETERAN REUNIONS AND THE GETTYSBURG BATTLEFIELD

Cohen, Stan. *Hands Across the Wall: The 50th and 75th Reunions of the Gettysburg Battle.* Pictorial Histories Publishing Company, Inc., 1982.

Davis, William C. *Gettysburg: The Story Behind the Scenery.* KC Publications, Inc., 1983.

Linenthal, Edward T. *Sacred Ground: Americans and Their Battlefields.* University of Illinois Press, 1993.

Test Your Knowledge Answer Key

CHAPTER 1

1. d. Breech, b. Muzzle, c. Breech, d. Muzzle, e. Muzzle, f. Breech
2. e.
3. d., e., b., a., c., f.
4. c.
5. c.
6. e.
7. larger
8. c.
9. a.
10. d.

CHAPTER 2

1. a. – 3, b. – 1, c. – 4, d. – 2
2. d.
3. b.
4. c.
5. b.
6. c., d., b., e., a.
7. b.
8. d.
9. a.
10. e.

CHAPTER 3

1. a.
2. c.
3. b.
4. e.
5. c.
6. d.
7. left
8. e.
9. b.
10. d.

CHAPTER 4

1. c.
2. a.
3. c.
4. b.
5. e.
6. b.
7. d.
8. d.
9. a., b., c.
10. d.

Extra Credit Answers

a. Chattanooga—14
b. Gettysburg—10
c. Second Bull Run—5
d. Atlanta Campaign—16
e. Siege of Vicksburg—11
f. First Bull Run—1
g. Hood's Tennessee Campaign—20
h. Antietam—6
i. *Monitor* vs. *Virginia*—2
j. Overland Campaign—15
k. Shiloh—3
l. Cedar Creek—18
m. Chickamauga—13
n. Seven Days—4
o. Fredericksburg—7
p. Chancellorsville—9
q. Stones River—8
r. March to the Sea—19
s. Siege of Petersburg—17
t. Fort Wagner—12

CHAPTER 5

1. c.
2. e.
3. e., d., b., c., a.
4. d.
5. c.
6. c.
7. a.
8. d.
9. a.
10. c.

CHAPTER 6

1. d.
2. c.
3. b.
4. e.
5. c.
6. a.
7. c.
8. c.
9. b.
10. a.

CHAPTER 7

1. b.
2. d.
3. c.
4. d.
5. e.
6. a. Confederate, b. Union, c. Union, d. Confederate, e. Union
7. e.
8. d.
9. b.
10. c.

CHAPTER 8

1. b.
2. d.
3. c.
4. e.
5. b.
6. c.
7. d.
8. d.
9. c.
10. d.

Endnotes

1. Darryl Lyman, *Civil War Quotations* (Conshohocken, PA, 1995), 41.

2. Mary Ashton Livermore, *My Story of the War* (Hartford, CT, 1890), 88–89.

3. Bell Irvin Wiley, *The Life of Billy Yank* (Baton Rouge, LA, 1981), 20.

4. Lyman, *Civil War Quotations*, 31.

5. Gregory Coco, *The Civil War Infantryman* (Gettysburg, PA, 1996), 6.

6. Robert L. Dabney, *The Life and Campaigns of Lieut.-Gen. Thomas J. Jackson* (New York, 1866), 251.

7. Leander Stillwell, *The Story of a Common Soldier of Army Life in the Civil War 1861–1865* (Franklin, TN, 1920), 15.

8. Thomas Frances Galwey, *The Valiant Hours* (Harrisburg, PA, 1961), 2.

9. Lyman, *Civil War Quotations*, 216.

10. Carlton McCarthy, *Detailed Minutiae of Soldier Life in the Army of Northern Virginia* (Richmond, 1899), 39.

11. John D. Billings, *Hardtack and Coffee or the Unwritten Story of Army Life* (Boston, 1887), 168–169.

12. *Ibid.*, 113–115.

13. McCarthy, *Detailed Minutiae of Soldier Life*, 28.

14. Robert U. Johnson and Clarence C. Buel, Eds., *Battles and Leaders of the Civil War* (New York, 1884, 1887, 1888), v. 2, 557–558.

15. *Ibid.*, v. 2, 662.

16. D. Augustus Dickert, *History of Kershaw's Brigade* (Newberry, SC, 1899), 237.

17. Ernest L. Linden, *History of the Nineteenth Regiment Massachusetts Volunteer Infantry* (Salem, MA, 1906), 181.

18. Lyman, *Civil War Quotations*, 233.

19. George B. McClellan, *McClellan's Own Story* (New York, 1887), 108.

20. William Fox, *Regimental Losses in the American Civil War* (Albany, 1898), 5.

21. Livermore, *My Story of the War*, 35–36.

22. Abner R. Small, *The Sixteenth Maine Regiment in the War of the Rebellion* (Portland, ME, 1886), 20.

23. Billings, *Hardtack and Coffee*, 270.

24. McClellan, *McClellan's Own Story*, 109–110.

25. Worthington C. Ford, *A Cycle of Adams Letters, 1861–1865* (Cambridge, MA, 1920), v. 2, 4.

26. John S. Mosby, *The Memoirs of Colonel John S. Mosby* (Boston, 1917), 30.

27. *The War of the Rebellion: A Compilation of the Official Records of the Union and Confederate Armies* (Washington, D.C., 1880–1901), v. 27, part 2, 680.

28. McClellan, *McClellan's Own Story*, 108–109.

29. Johnson and Buel, *Battles and Leaders*, v. 3, 79.

30. *Ibid.*, v. 3, 81.

31. *Atlantic Monthly* (Cambridge, MA, 1911), v. 108, 221.

32. Earl J. Hess, *Pickett's Charge—The Last Attack at Gettysburg* (Chapel Hill, NC, 2000), 315.

33. Dabney, *The Life and Campaigns of Lieut.-Gen. Thomas J. Jackson*, 222.

34. *Ibid.*, 222.

35. *Ibid.*, 222.

36. Frances Kennedy, *The Civil War Battlefield Guide* (Boston, 1998), 13–421; Thomas Livermore, *Numbers and Losses in the Civil War* (New York, 1900), 77–136.

37. Johnson and Buel, *Battles and Leaders*, v. 1, 692.

38. Jacques W. Redway, *The Making of the Empire State* (New York, 1904), 207.

39. Johnson and Buel, *Battles and Leaders*, v. 1, 474.

40. William P. Johnston, *The Life of Gen. Albert Sidney Johnston* (New York, 1879), 658.

41. Lyman, *Civil War Quotations*, 168.

42. *Ibid*, 168.

43. Johnson and Buel, *Battles and Leaders*, v. 2, 489.

44. John Gibbon, *Personal Recollections of the Civil War* (New York, 1928), 73.

45. Johnson and Buel, *Battles and Leaders*, v. 2, 605–606.

46. Walter H. Taylor, "General Lee: His Campaigns in Virginia" (Norfolk, VA, 1906), 126.

47. Arthur B. Lapsley, Ed., *The Works of Abraham Lincoln* (New York, 1906), v. 6, 223.

48. Galwey, *The Valiant Hours*, 63.

49. Johnson and Buel, *Battles and Leaders*, v. 3, 82.

50. Lapsley, *The Works of Abraham Lincoln*, v. 6, 223.

51. Johnson and Buel, *Battles and Leaders*, v. 3, 634.

52. *The War of the Rebellion: A Compilation of the Official Records of the Union and Confederate Armies*, v. 20, part 1, 784.

53. George W. Brent, *Diary*, January 2, 1863, Palmer Collection of Bragg Papers, Western Reserve Historical Society.

54. Lapsley, *The Works of Abraham Lincoln*, v. 6, 424.

55. Helen Nicolay, *Personal Traits of Abraham Lincoln* (New York, 1912), 34.

56. Robert Edward Lee, *Recollections and Letters of General Robert E. Lee* (New York, 1905), 93.

57. John Bigelow, Jr., *The Campaign of Chancellorsville* (New Haven, CT, 1910), 108.

58. Johnson and Buel, *Battles and Leaders*, v. 3, 195.

59. Wayne Whipple, *The Story-Life of Lincoln* (Philadelphia, 1908), 510.

60. Edward A. Pollard, *Lee and His Lieutenants* (New York, 1867), 123.

61. Mary Anna Jackson, *Life and Letters of General Thomas J. Jackson (Stonewall Jackson)* (New York, 1892), 471.

62. William Faulkner, *Intruder in the Dust* (New York, 1991), 190.

63. Johnson and Buel, *Battles and Leaders*, v. 3, 284.

64. *Ibid.*, v. 3, 329.

65. *Ibid.*, v. 3, 342–343.

66. *Ibid.*, v. 3, 342–343.

67. *Ibid.*, v. 3, 345.

68. *Ibid.*, v. 3, 347.

69. Charles C. Coffin, *Marching to Victory* (New York, 1916), 303.

70. Terrence Winschel, *Vicksburg: Fall of the Confederate Gibraltar* (Abilene, TX, 1999), 14.

71. Hosea W. Rood, *Wisconsin at Vicksburg* (Madison, WI, 1914), 336.

72. Ulysses S. Grant, *Personal Memoirs of U. S. Grant* (New York, 1885), v. 1, 422.

73. John Nicolay and John Hay, Eds., *Complete Works of Abraham Lincoln* (New York, 1905), v. 12, 47.

74. Paul and Stephen Kendrick, *Douglass and Lincoln* (New York, 2008), 138.

75. *Harper's New Monthly Magazine* (New York, 1865), v. 30, 435.

76. William A. Sinclair, *The Aftermath of Slavery* (Boston, 1905), 27.

77. Thomas F. Porter, *City Songs and Country Carols* (Boston, 1906), 66.

78. William H. Venable, Editor, *Poems of William Haines Lytle* (Cincinnati, OH, 1894), 35.

79. Byron A. Dunn, *On General Thomas's Staff* (Chicago, 1899), 344.

80. *The War of the Rebellion: A Compilation of the Official Records of the Union and Confederate Armies* , v. 30, part 1, 141.

81. *Ibid.*, v. 30, part 1, 142–143.

82. *Ibid.*, v. 30, part 2, 150.

83. *Ibid.*, v. 31, part 2, 682.

84. *Ibid.*, v. 30, part 4, 706.

85. Joseph Morton, Jr., Editor, *Sparks from the Camp Fire or Tales of the Old Veterans* (Philadelphia, 1899), 441.

86. *The War of the Rebellion: A Compilation of the Official Records of the Union and Confederate Armies*, v. 52, part 21, 745.

87. Earl Schenck Miers, *Robert E. Lee, a Great Life in Brief* (New York, 1956), 171.

88. *National Park Service, Fredericksburg Battlefields: Official National Park Handbook* (Washington, D.C., 2000), 51.

89. Johnson and Buel, *Battles and Leaders*, v. 4, 154.

90. Grant, *Personal Memoirs*, v. 2, 215.

91. David King, A. Judson Gibbs, and Jay Northup, Editors, *History of the Ninety-Third Regiment, New York Volunteer Infantry* (Milwaukee, WI, 1895), 447–448.

92. Reverend J. William Jones, *Personal Reminiscences, Anecdotes, and Letters of Gen. Robert E. Lee* (New York, 1875), 41.

93. Grant, *Personal Memoirs*, v. 2, 276.

94. Miers, *Robert E. Lee*, 171.

95. Jones, *Personal Reminiscences*, 41.

96. *Augusta Daily Constitutionalist*, May 1, 1864.

97. Johnson and Buel, *Battles and Leaders*, v. 4, 250.

98. Grant, *Personal Memoirs*, v. 2, 131.

99. *Ibid.*, v. 2, 131.

100. Ambrose Bierce, *The Collected Works of Ambrose Bierce* (New York, 1909), v. 1, 279.

101. William T. Sherman, *Memoirs of General William T. Sherman* (New York, 1875), v. 2, 59–60.

102. Johnson and Buel, *Battles and Leaders*, v. 4, 253.

103. *Ibid.*, v. 4, 252–253.

104. *Augusta Daily Constitutionalist*, May 1, 1864.

105. Johnson and Buel, *Battles and Leaders*, v. 4, 253.

106. *Ibid.*, v. 4, 254.

107. *The War of the Rebellion: A Compilation of the Official Records of the Union and Confederate Armies*, v. 40, part 1, 17.

108. *The War of the Rebellion: A Compilation of the Official Records of the Union and Confederate Armies*, v. 37, part 2, 300–301.

109. *Report of the Proceedings of the Society of the Army of the Tennessee at the Twenty-First Meeting* (Cincinnati, OH, 1893), 78.

110. *Ibid.*, 78.

111. *Ibid.*, 78–79.

112. Benson J. Lossing, *Pictorial History of the Civil War* (Hartford, CT, 1877), v. 3, 366.

113. Charles C. Coffin, *Four Years of Fighting: A Volume of Personal Observation with the Army and Navy* (Boston, 1866), 392.

114. Sherman, *Memoirs of General William T. Sherman*, v. 2, 126.

115. *Ibid.*, v. 2, 14–15.

116. *Ibid.*, v. 2, 231.

117. Sam R. Watkins, *"Co. Aytch," Maury Grays, First Tennessee Regiment* (Chattanooga, TN, 1900), 218.

118. Levi T. Scofield, *The Retreat from Pulaski to Nashville, Tenn.* (Cleveland, OH, 1909), 21.

119. John Nicholay and John Hay, Eds., *Complete Works of Abraham Lincoln* (New York, 1894), v. 2, 672.

120. Grant, *Personal Memoirs*, v. 2, 489.

121. James Longstreet, *From Manassas to Appomattox* (Philadelphia, 1896), 615.

122. *Ibid.*, 624.

123. Johnson and Buel, *Battles and Leaders*, v. 4, 747.

124. McCarthy, *Detailed Minutiae of Soldier Life in the Army of Northern Virginia*, 157.

125. Jacob D. Cox, *Military Reminiscences of the Civil War* (New York, 1900), v. 2, 531–532.

126. Johnson and Buel, *Battles and Leaders*, v. 4, 756.

127. *Ibid.*, v. 4, 756.

128. *Ibid.*, v. 4, 757.

129. *The War of the Rebellion: A Compilation of the Official Records of the Union and Confederate Armies*, v. 47, 1061.

130. Charles H. Kirk, *History of the Fifteenth Pennsylvania Volunteer Cavalry* (Philadelphia, 1906), 509.

131. Jefferson Davis, *The Rise and Fall of the Confederate Government* (New York, 1881), v. 2, 701.

132. C. W. Raines, Editor, *Six Decades in Texas or Memoirs of Francis Richard Lubbock* (Austin, TX, 1900), 572.

133. Rev. J. William Jones, *Southern Historical Society Papers*, v. 6, July to December 1878, 165.

134. William T. Sherman, *Address to Grand Army of the Republic, Columbus, Ohio, August 11, 1880*.

135. Walt Whitman, *Specimen Days and Collect* (Philadelphia, 1882–83), 81.

136. Fox, *Regimental Losses in the American Civil War*, 525–535; Livermore, *Numbers and Losses in the Civil War*, 14–48.

137. Frank Moore, editor, *The Rebellion Record: A Diary of American Events, with Documents, Narratives, Illustrative Incidents, Poetry, etc.* (New York, 1862), v. 3, 71.

138. William H. Price, *Civil War Handbook* (Springfield, VA, 1961), 69.

139. Sherman, *Memoirs of General William T. Sherman*, v. 2, 385

140. Fox, *Regimental Losses in the American Civil War*, 36; Robert C. Wood, *Confederate Hand-Book* (New Orleans, LA, 1900), 36.

141. *The Century Illustrated Monthly Magazine* (New York, 1887), v. 33, 309.

142. Johnson and Buel, *Battles and Leaders*, v. 4, 175.

143. Fox, *Regimental Losses in the American Civil War*, 40–42 and 571–573.

144. Grant, *Personal Memoirs*, v. 2, 40.

145. Mary Boykin Chestnut, *A Diary from Dixie* (New York, 1905), 284.

146. *The War of the Rebellion: A Compilation of the Official Records of the Union and Confederate Armies*, series 2, v. 7, 607.

147. *Ibid.*, series 2, v. 4, 267.

148. Lonnie Speer, *Portals to Hell* (Lincoln, NE, 2005), 323–340.

149. John L. Ransom, *Andersonville Diary, Escape, and List of the Dead* (Auburn, NY, 1881), 78

150. John McElroy, *Andersonville: A Story of Rebel Military Prisons* (Washington, 1913), 117.

151. Joseph K. Barnes, *Medical and Surgical History of the War of the Rebellion* (Washington, DC, 1870–1888), part 3, v.1, 35.

152. Griffin Frost, *Camp and Prison Journal* (Quincy, IL, 1867), 276.

153. Barnes, *Medical and Surgical History of the War of the Rebellion*, part 3, v.1, 46.

154. Louis Beaudry, *The Libby Chronicle: Devoted to Facts and Fun* (Albany, NY, 1889), 22.

155. _____, "The Richmond Prisoners." *New York Herald*, November 28, 1863.

156. Walter Clark, Editor, *Histories of the Several Regiments and Battalions from North Carolina* (Goldsboro, NC, 1901), v. 4, 667–668.

157. *The War of the Rebellion: A Compilation of the Official Records of the Union and Confederate Armies*, series 2, v. 8, 330.

158. Barnes, *Medical and Surgical History of the War of the Rebellion*, part 3, v.1, 46.

159. Mrs. B. A. C. Emerson, *Historic Southern Monuments* (New York, 1911), 328.

160. *Confederate Veteran Magazine* (Nashville, TN, June 1895), v. 3, Number 6, 183

161. *Ibid.*, v. 3, Number 6, 182.

162. *Ibid.*, v. 3, Number 6, 183.

163. *Ibid.*, v. 3, Number 6, 183.

164. Noah Brooks, *Washington in Lincoln's Time* (New York, 1895), 38.

165. Rev. J. William Jones, *Christ in Camp or Religion in Lee's Army* (Richmond, VA, 1887), 401.

166. *Ibid.*, 400.

167. *Ibid.*, 401.

168. *Ibid.*, 401.

169. Ambrose Bierce, *In the Midst of Life: Tales of Soldiers and Civilians* (New York, 1898), 15.

170. *Indianapolis Journal*, July 27, 1861.

171. Ambrose Bierce, *The Collected Works of Ambrose Bierce*, v. 1, 244.

172. *Ibid.*, v. 1, 255.

173. *San Francisco Examiner*, August 17, 1890.

174. Mrs. C. Emma Cheney, *Young Folks' History of the Civil War* (Boston, 1884), 403.

175. *Belmont Chronicle*, April 28, 1864.

176. Charles Robbins deposition, January 18, 1893, during John Crapsey's request for payment of Angelo Crapsey's pension. Dennis Brandt, *Pathway to Hell: A Tragedy of the American Civil War* (Lincoln, NE, 2008), 116.

177. William Pittenger, *The Great Locomotive Chase: A History of Andrews Railroad Raid into Georgia in 1862* (New York, 1893), 464.

178. S. W. Butler and R. J. Levis, Eds., *Medical and Surgical Reporter: A Weekly Journal* (Philadelphia, 1862), v. 7, 184.

179. Stephen Vincent Benet, *John Brown's Body* (New York, 1928), Book 7.

180. *Report of the President of Bowdoin College for the Academic Year*, 1913–1914 (Brunswick, ME, 1914), 6.

181. Pennsylvania Commission, *Fiftieth Anniversary of the Battle of Gettysburg* (Harrisburg, PA, 1913), 115.

182. Martin Blumenson and George Smith Patton, *The Patton Papers: 1885–1940* (New York, 1972), 173.

183. *Report of the President of Bowdoin College for the Academic Year, 1913–1914*, 6.

About the National Civil War Museum

Located in Harrisburg, Pennsylvania, The National Civil War Museum sits strategically above the Susquehanna Valley. The Museum incorporates collections of artifacts, manuscripts, documents, photographs, and other printed matter that exceed 24,000 items. Although many items have been donated to The National Civil War Museum since its opening, the vast majority of its collections were acquired by the City of Harrisburg between 1994 and 1999 under the auspices of Mayor Stephen R. Reed.

The National Civil War Museum's mission encompasses the period from 1850 through 1876, and its collections vary widely in scope and years of manufacture. The Museum's mission is to serve as a national center to inspire lifelong learning of the American Civil War through the preservation and balanced presentation of the American peoples struggles for survival and healing.

For information, please visit www.nationalcivilwarmuseum.org.

Index

246